Shoe
Comn

Shoe-Leather Commitment

J. Oswald Sanders

MOODY PRESS
CHICAGO

ISBN: 0-8024-3104-6

1 2 3 4 5 6 7 8 Printing/BC/Year 95 94 93 92 91 90

Printed in the United States of America

CONTENTS

INTRODUCTION

The initial call of Christ to the men with whom He planned to associate in His purpose of world evanzelization was a call to discipleship.

> As Jesus walked beside the Sea of Galilee, He saw Simon and his brother Andrew casting a net into the lake, for they were fishermen. *"Come, follow me,"* Jesus said, "and I will make you fishers of men."
>
> (Mark 1:16-17; italics added)

His charisma was such that "at once they left their nets and followed Him" (v. 18). In the ensuing days He gave the same call to others.

After He rose from the dead, but before He ascended to heaven, Jesus gave to these same men (and to us) the command "Go, and *make disciples* of all nations," adding the assurance "Surely I am with you always, to the very end of the age" (Matthew 28:19-20; italics added). This is the true calling and function of the church. It is the privilege and responsibility of the whole church to respond in obedience and give the whole gospel to the whole world.

Today discipleship is a standard subject for study in churches and groups. Seminars on discipleship abound, and there is no question of the importance of the subject.

But when the lives of many Christians are put alongside the life-style Jesus prescribed for disciples, and demonstrated Himself, there is a vast discrepancy. It is one thing to master the biblical principles of discipleship, but quite another to transfer those principles into common shoe-leather.

It is not without significance that the word *disciple* occurs in the New Testament 269 times, *Christian* only 3 times, and *believers* 2 times. This surely indicates that the task of the church is not so much to make "Christians" or "believers" but "disciples." A disciple must, of course, be a believer; but according to Christ's conditions of discipleship (Luke 14:25-33), not all believers are disciples of the New Testament stamp.

The word *disciple* means "a learner," but Jesus infused into that simple word a wealth of profound meaning. As used by Him and by Paul, it means "a learner or pupil who accepts the teaching of Christ, not only in belief but also in life-style." This involves acceptance of the views and practice of the Teacher. In other words, it means learning with the purpose to obey what is learned. It involves a deliberate choice, a definite denial, and a determined obedience.

Today one may be regarded as a Christian even if there are few, if any, signs of progress in discipleship. It was not so in the early church. Then discipleship involved the kind of commitment Peter spoke about when he protested to the Lord, "We have left everything to follow you!" (Mark 10:28).

The temper of our times is for instant gratification and short-term commitment—quick answers to prayer and quick results with a minimum of effort and discomfort. But there is no such thing as easy and instant discipleship. One can commence a walk of discipleship in a moment, but the first step must lengthen into a life-long walk. There is no such thing as short-term discipleship.

To some who have been nurtured on the "easy believism" doctrine, the radical demands of Christ may seem excessive and unreasonable. The result is that after they have traveled a short distance, and the path grows more steep and rugged, they are like the disciples mentioned in John 6:66: "From that time many of His disciples turned back and no longer followed Him." He is looking for men and women of quality for whom there is no turning back.

In this book I have not dealt with the mechanics of discipleship but rather with its standards—the underlying principles that are to be incorporated into the lifestyle of the disciple. There is also encouragement for those who have failed in this area to step out again.

1
THE IDEAL DISCIPLE

"Blessed are you . . . " (Matthew 5:11).

It is more than a coincidence that whereas the last word of the Old Testament, which enshrines the Old Covenant, is "curse," the first word of our Lord's first recorded sermon under the New Covenant is "blessed." This latter word is the keynote of His kingdom.

The Old Covenant of law could pronounce only a curse on those who failed to fulfill its demands. The New Covenant, which was sealed with Christ's blood, does not reduce the law's demands but imparts the desire and the dynamic to fulfill them. The "thou shalt, thou shalt not" of the Old is replaced by the "I will, I will" of the New.

In the Beatitudes (Matthew 5:3-12), Jesus set forth the characteristics of the ideal subjects of His kingdom —qualities that were present in perfection in the life and character of the One who announced them. It is a fascinating exercise to match each of those virtues to the life and ministry of the Lord.

In His Sermon on the Mount Jesus addressed His words primarily to His disciples but did so in the hearing of the crowd (v. 1). "His disciples came to him, and he began to teach them." So this is a message for disciples.

He directed their attention away from the idea of being satisfied with mere outward presentability to an immeasurably higher and more demanding life-style.

The standard He set is so high that no one can live the life depicted in the Sermon who is not the one depicted in the Beatitudes. The whole Sermon is revolutionary, but nowhere more so than in these verses. They cut right across the popular idea of the definition of blessedness and happiness.

Many think that if they had abundant wealth, absence of sorrow and suffering, good health, a good job, unrestricted gratification of appetites, and kind treatment from everyone, that would be blessedness indeed. But Jesus completely reversed that concept and substituted many of the very experiences we would like to sidestep—poverty, mourning, hunger, thirst, renunciation, persecution. True blessedness is to be found along this path, He told them.

The word *blessed* can be rendered "O the bliss!" or "to be envied, to be congratulated," and it is applied to eight conditions of life that divide into two groups.

Four Passive Personal Qualities

Christ begins by calling four passive personal qualities blessed.

Spiritual Inadequacy

"Blessed are the poor in spirit, for theirs is the kingdom of heaven" (v. 3), or "O the bliss of those who feel inadequate!"

On the surface those words have a hollow ring to those whose lives are plagued by that debilitating condition. Of course it is to the poor in spirit that our Lord is referring here, not to the poor in pocket. There is no virtue in poverty per se; it is certainly not an automatic blessing.

There are two words for "poor" in Greek. One means someone who has nothing superfluous; the other, one who has nothing at all, is bankrupt, and has no resources. It is this second meaning that Jesus referred to. The lesson is clear. The person who is to be envied is the one who, in consciousness of his spiritual bankruptcy, is cast back on God and draws on His limitless resources. As Luther said, "We are all beggars, living on the bounty of God." But such poverty leads to spiritual affluence. "Theirs is the kingdom of heaven."

SPIRITUAL CONTRITION

"Blessed are those who mourn for they will be comforted" (v. 4), or "O the bliss of the penitent!"

This is another paradox. It is as though one said, "How happy are the unhappy!" This quality is the product of the poverty of spirit of the first beatitude. It is not bereavement that is primarily in view, although that need not be excluded. The word *mourn* conveys the idea of grief of the deepest kind. It is mourning over sin and failure, over the slowness of our growth in likeness to Christ—mourning over our spiritual bankruptcy.

There are two mistakes that the disciple may make. One is to believe that Christians must never be happy and laughing; the other, that Christians must always be happy and laughing. As a wise man said, "There is a time for everything . . . a time to weep and a time to laugh, a time to mourn and a time to dance" (Ecclesiastes 3:1, 4).

No one attains full maturity without the experience of sorrow. There is room for the disciple to mourn over the slowness of his growth and the paucity of his spiritual attainment altogether apart from any actual sin in his life.

Mourning and bliss are not incompatible, for Jesus said, "Blessed are you who weep now, for you will laugh" (Luke 6:21). The blessedness is in the comfort God gives, not in the mourning itself. "They will be comforted."

SPIRITUAL HUMILITY

"Blessed are the meek for they will inherit the earth" (v. 5), or "O the bliss of the humble!"

Humility is an exotic flower in our sooty and smoggy world. It is no native of earth and is little esteemed by man in general.

The word *meek* is more than amicability or mere mildness of disposition. Its meaning has been weakened by the line in the children's hymn "Gentle Jesus, meek and mild." He was meek but was far from mild. The impression the hymn leaves is that Jesus was rather weak and ineffective. In fact, He was the very reverse of weak.

Was it mildness He displayed when, alone and with uplifted whip, He drove the materialistic traffickers with their sheep and cattle out of the Temple? He was anything but servile and spineless. When He asked the disciples who men said that He was, they replied,"Some say Elijah, some John the Baptist"—two of the most rugged characters in the Bible! The word *meek* was used of a horse that had been broken and domesticated, giving the idea of energy and power, controlled and directed.

In heaven, the seven angels sing the Song of Moses and the Lamb (Revelation 15:3)—Moses, the meekest man on earth, and Jesus who said, "I am meek and lowly in heart." But both could blaze with sinless anger when the interests of God were at stake. Meekness is no spineless quality.

This virtue challenges the world's standards. "Stand up for your rights!" is the strident cry of our day. "The world is yours if you can get it." Jesus said, on the contrary, that the world is yours if you renounce it. The meek, not the aggressive, inherit the earth. The meek have an inheritance. The worldly have no future. "They will inherit the earth."

SPIRITUAL ASPIRATION

"Blessed are those who hunger and thirst for righteousness for they will be filled" (v. 6), or "O the bliss of the unsatisfied."

The blessing promised here is not for mere wistfulness or languid desire. It is for those who have a passionate craving not after happiness alone but after righteousness—a right relationship with God. The truly blessed person is the one who hungers and thirsts after God Himself, not only the blessings He gives. David knew that aspiration when he wrote, "As the deer pants for streams of water, so my soul pants for you, O God" (Psalm 42:1).

The discovery that happiness is a by-product of holiness has been a joyous revelation to many. We should therefore "follow after holiness." God is eager to satisfy all the holy aspirations of His children. "They will be filled."

FOUR ACTIVE SOCIAL QUALITIES

The ideal disciple will have four active social characteristics.

COMPASSIONATE IN SPIRIT

"Blessed are the merciful, for they will be shown mercy" (v. 7), or "O the bliss of the merciful!"

It is always to the undeserving that mercy is extended. If it were deserved, it would no longer be mercy but mere justice.

It is possible to have a passion for righteousness and yet lack compassion and mercy for those who have failed to attain it. Mercy is the ability to enter into another's situation and be sympathetic toward his plight or problem. Like meekness, this is a distinctively Christian grace. We are naturally geared more to criticism than to mercy.

Pity can be sterile. To become mercy, it must graduate from mere emotion to compassionate action. Although mercy does not condone sin, it endeavors to repair its ravages. Mercy encourages the one who has fallen to begin again.

Our personal experience will be the rebound of our attitudes and reactions. Just as in physics, where action and reaction are equal and opposite—those who are merciful will be shown mercy, and if we are shown mercy, we will be merciful. "They will be shown mercy."

PURE IN HEART

"Blessed are the pure in heart, for they will see God" (v. 8), or "O the bliss of the sincere!"

Cleanness of heart brings clearness of vision. The emphasis here is on inward purity and reality in contrast to external respectability.

The revelation of God envisaged here is not granted to the mighty intellect unless that is accompanied by purity of heart. It is more than an intellectual concept that is in view; it is not a matter of optics but of moral and spiritual affinity. Sin befogs the vision. The word *pure* here means "unadulterated," free from alloy, sincere and without hypocrisy. "They will see God."

CONCILIATORY IN SPIRIT

"Blessed are the peacemakers, for they will be called sons of God" (v. 9), or "O the bliss of those who create harmony!"

It is not peace-lovers or peacekeepers who qualify for this beatitude, but peacemakers. Nor is it those who maintain an existing peace, but those who enter a situation where peace has been broken and restore it. The beatitude speaks not of a pacifist but of a reconciler.

Very often peace can be made only at a cost to the peacemaker himself. It was so with our Lord. "He made peace by the blood of His cross." He achieved it by allowing His own peace to be broken. The disciple is to follow in His train. To be a lover of peace is good. To be a promoter of peace is better. "They will be called sons of God."

UNSWERVING IN LOYALTY

"Blessed are those who are persecuted because of righteousness, for theirs is the kingdom of heaven. Blessed are you when people insult you, persecute you and falsely say all kinds of evil against you because of me. Rejoice and be glad, because great is your reward in heaven" (vv. 10-11), or "O the bliss of the sufferer for Christ."

What was done to the Savior will be done to the disciple. But even insult, reviling, injury, and persecution can work blessing—not in the persecution itself but in the divine compensations it brings.

The tense of the verb conveys the sense, "Blessed are those who *have been* persecuted." The blessing is in the results that flow from it. Suffering is the authentic hallmark of Christianity. "Even if you should suffer for what is right, you are blessed," said Peter (1 Peter 3:14).

But not all persecution is blessed. Sometimes Christians bring it on themselves through unwise and unchristian actions. For persecution to bring blessing, there are three conditions:

(1) It must be for righteousness' sake, not as a result of our angularity or fanaticism or tactlessness.

(2) The evil-speaking must have no basis in fact; it must not be something that is the outcome of our sin or failure.

(3) It must be for Christ's sake—suffering that arises from our consistent loyalty to Him.

"Great is your reward in heaven."

2
CONDITIONS OF DISCIPLESHIP

"Anyone who does not carry his cross and follow me cannot be my disciple" (Luke 14:27).

As usual, Jesus was surrounded by the thronging crowds, who were listening to His every word. "Large crowds were traveling with Jesus" (Luke 14:25), fascinated by the novelty, winsomeness, and challenge of this new teaching, for it was still in the days of His popularity.

The situation presented Him with a unique opportunity to capitalize on their feverish interest. The whole nation was looking for a charismatic leader who would help them throw off the galling Roman yoke—and here was someone superbly qualified for the task. All He needed to do was to perform a few spectacular miracles and then lead them in a great insurrection.

Did He flatter them, offer some inducement, perform some miracle to win their allegiance? It seemed as though He were intent on alienating their interest and actually discouraging them from following Him. He began to thin their ranks by stating in the starkest of terms the exacting conditions of discipleship.

The line Jesus took with the impressionable crowd was the exact opposite of much evangelical evangelism today. Instead of majoring in the benefits and blessings, the thrills and excitement, the adventure and advantages of being His disciples, He spoke more of the difficulties and dangers they would meet and the sacrifices that would be involved. He placed the cost of being His disciple very high. He never concealed the cross.

Robert Browning captures this aspect of the Lord's message in one of his poems:

> How very hard it is to be a Christian!
> Hard for you and me,
> Not for the mere task of making real
> That duty up to its ideal,
> Effecting thus complete and whole
> A purpose of the human soul,
> For that is always hard to do.

It is a well-proved fact that dynamic leaders in all ages and in all spheres have always met with the best response when they confronted people with the difficult challenge rather than the soft option. The appeal to self-interest inevitably draws the wrong kind of follower.

In the early stages of World War II, when the highly mechanized German armies were sweeping forward almost unchecked, the French resistance collapsed. Great Britain was left alone with its "contemptible army" on foreign soil to face alone the German colossus.

I well remember a speech by Prime Minister Winston Churchill at that critical juncture. It outlined in starkest terms the ominous situation in which the nation was placed, with inadequate weapons, weak defenses, and the possibility of an invasion imminent. He uttered no soft words of comfort but challenged the whole nation to rise to the occasion.

> We will fight them on the streets;
> We will fight them on the beaches . . .
> All I offer you is blood and sweat and tears.

Instead of depressing them, his words galvanized the nation into a superhuman war effort that turned the tide and won the day.

Why did Jesus impose such stringent terms? Had He been prepared to soften His conditions of discipleship the crowds would have swept along behind Him, but that was not His way. He was looking for men and women of quality; mere quantity did not interest Him.

In His message to the crowds concerning the conditions on which they could be His disciples, Jesus employed two illustrations:

> Suppose one of you wants to build a tower. Will he not first sit down and estimate the cost to see if he has enough money to complete it? . . . Or suppose a king is about to go to war against another king. Will he not first sit down and consider whether he is able with ten thousand men to oppose the one coming against him with twenty thousand? (Luke 14:28, 31)

Jesus employed these illustrations to demonstrate His disapproval of impulsive and ill-considered discipleship. Like the builder, He too is engaged in a building program—"On this rock I will build my church" (Matthew 16:18). Like the king, He too is engaged in a desperate battle against the devil and the powers of darkness.

In this building and battling, Jesus desires to have associated with Him disciples who are men and women of quality—those who will not turn back when the fighting grows fierce. Are we disciples of this caliber?

The message Jesus proclaimed was a call to discipleship—not to faith alone but to faith and obedience. Jesus gave a solemn warning: "Not everyone who says to me, 'Lord, Lord,' will enter the kingdom of heaven" (Matthew 7:21). Obedience is evidence of the reality of our repentance and faith. Our obedience does not achieve salvation, but it is evidence of it.

Present-day preaching finds little place for repentance, yet without repentance there can be no regeneration. Many have been encouraged to believe that because they have come forward to an appeal or signed a decision card, or prayed to receive Christ, they are saved—whether or not there is any subsequent change in their lives.

It needs to be reiterated that "saving faith is more than just understanding the facts [of the gospel] and mentally acquiescing. It is inseparable from repentance, submission, and a supernatural eagerness to obey. The biblical concept of saving faith includes all those elements."

It is sad but true that whenever the way of the cross and its implications are preached superficial believers, whose conversion experiences have been shallow, fall away.

There are three indispensable conditions for true discipleship:

AN UNRIVALED LOVE

The first condition of discipleship is an unrivaled love for Christ. In the realm of the disciple's affections He will allow no rival.

The reader will have noticed that in Luke 14:25-33 one statement is repeated three times: "he cannot be my disciple." Each occurrence of the clause is preceded by a condition to which there is no exception.

> If anyone comes to me and does not hate his father and mother, his wife and children, his brothers and sisters —yes, even his own life—*he cannot be my disciple* (v. 26).
>
> Anyone who loves his father or mother more than me is not worthy of me (Matthew 10:37; italics added).

The use of the word *hate* here has been the cause of considerable misunderstanding. The word Christ used is far removed from the normal connotation of the word in today's usage. He does not tell us in one breath to love and honor our parents and then in the next to hate them. Jesus was using the language of exaggerated contrast. *Hate* here means simply "to love less." So the disciple is a follower of Christ whose love for Him transcends all earthly loves.

But note that because we love Christ supremely does not mean we will love our relatives less than we love them now. Indeed, the very reverse can be the case; for when Christ holds first place in our affections, our capacity to love will be greatly expanded. Romans 5:5 will then have a fuller meaning for us: "God has poured out his love into our hearts by the Holy Spirit, whom he has given us."

Sometimes a clash of loyalties arises at this point, and the disciple must choose which love will prevail.

When the China Inland Mission (now Overseas Missionary Fellowship) had to withdraw from China, one of the countries to which they transferred operations was Thailand. The mission was assigned several provinces with a population of about 4 million in which there were no churches and no missionary work.

In one town, the first to be converted was a high school girl named Si Muang. Her heart opened to the gospel as a flower opens to the sun. She soon realized that she had to confess her faith in Christ to her parents, who were ardent Buddhists. She was under no illusions as to the possible outcome.

Overcoming her fears, she confessed her faith to her mother. Her mother was furious and told Si Muang that she must either renounce this new religion or leave home —a painful dilemma for a young girl to face, especially as she was the only Christian in the town. The conflict was fierce. Would she give Christ an unrivaled love and "hate" her father and mother, brothers and sisters? That is what she did, and she was turned out of her home. The Lord did not desert her, and some months later she was received back.

There was yet another area that came under this condition of discipleship: "Yes, even his own life." The disciple's love for Christ is to be supreme over self-love. We are not to hold even our own lives dear. Love of self is soul-destroying, but love of Christ is soul-enriching. If the disciple is not prepared to comply with this condition, the words are categorical: "He cannot be my disciple" (v. 26).

An Unceasing Cross-Bearing

"Anyone who does not carry his cross and follow me *cannot be my disciple*" (Luke 14:27; italics added).

"Anyone who does not take his cross and follow me *is not worthy of me*" (Matthew 10:38; italics added).

To understand what Jesus meant by His command to carry the cross, we must think what that expression would have meant to the people of that day.

What is the cross of which Jesus spoke? Those words were said before He went to the cross. In common parlance people speak of some physical infirmity, some temperamental weakness, some family problem, as their cross. One woman referred to her bad temper as her cross.

"Oh, no!" was the reply. "That is the cross of the unfortunate people who have to live with you."

Those are not the circumstances the Jews would have associated with a cross—they are just the common lot of man. Crucifixion was an all too familiar sight to them. They would have thought of the cross as an instrument of agonizing suffering and eventual death.

What did the cross mean to Jesus? It was something He took up voluntarily, not something that was imposed on Him; it involved sacrifice and suffering; it involved Him in costly renunciations; it was symbolic of rejection by the world.

And it is to cross-bearing of this nature that the disciple is always called. It involves a willingness to accept ostracism and unpopularity with the world for His sake. We can evade carrying the cross simply by conforming our lives to the world's standards.

Contrary to expectation, taking our cross and following Christ is not a joyless experience, as the saintly Samuel Rutherford knew: "He who looks at the white side of Christ's cross, and takes it up handsomely, will find it just such a burden as wings are to a bird."

If the disciple is unwilling to fulfill this condition, Jesus said, "He cannot be my disciple."

AN UNRESERVED SURRENDER

"Any of you who does not give up everything he has cannot be my disciple" (Luke 14:33).

The first condition had to do with the heart's affections; the second with life's conduct; the third with personal possessions. Of the three, the third condition is probably the most unwelcome of all in our covetous and materialistic age. Did Jesus mean what He said to be taken literally? Everything?

What was the Lord really asking for? I do not think He meant that we are to sell all that we have and give it to the church, but He was claiming the right of disposal of our possessions. He has given them to us only as trustees, not as owners.

This was the test Jesus put to the young man who came inquiring about eternal life: "Jesus answered, 'If you want to be perfect, go, sell your possessions and give to the poor, and you will have treasure in heaven. *Then come,* follow me'" (Matthew 19:21; italics added). He had to choose between Christ and his many possessions. He flunked the test, and because he was unwilling to forsake all, he disqualified himself from being a disciple of Christ. Christ must be given preeminence over all earthly possessions.

There are two ways in which we can hold our possessions. We can hold them in our clenched fist and say, "These are mine to do with as I like." Or we can hold them with our hand inverted, the fingers lightly touching, and say, "Thank you, Lord, for loaning me these possessions. I realize I am only a trustee, not an owner. If you want any of them back again, tell me, and I will let them go." The latter is the attitude of the disciple.

Our attitude toward our possessions is a clue to the reality of our discipleship. When we are thinking of our stewardship of money, what is our attitude? Is it, "How much of my money will I give to God?" Or is it, "How much of God's money will I keep for myself?"

In view of the stringency of those conditions, it may be asked, "Has the Lord the right to demand them as conditions of discipleship?" The answer is that He is asking nothing that He has not first done Himself.

Did He not love His Father supremely, more than He loved mother, brothers, sisters, and His own life also?

Did He not carry and die on a literal, agonizing cross to secure our salvation?

Did He not renounce all that He had as heir of all things? When He died, His personal estate consisted of the loincloth that the soldiers left Him after gambling away His outer garments.

> Jesus, I my cross have taken,
> All to leave and follow Thee;
> Destitute, despised, forsaken,
> Thou, from hence, my all shalt be:

I will follow Thee, my Saviour
Thou didst shed Thy blood for me,
And though all the world forsake Thee,
By Thy grace I'll follow Thee.

(H. F. Lyte)

3
EVIDENCES OF DISCIPLESHIP

"By this all men will know that you are my disciples, if you love one another" (John 13:35).

It is significant that Jesus did not command His followers to go and make believers, or converts, of all nations. His clear, unequivocal command was: "All authority in heaven and on earth has been given to me. Therefore *go and make disciples of all nations"* (Matthew 28:18-19; italics added).

A disciple is simply "a learner." The word comes from a root that means "thought accompanied by endeavor." So a disciple of Christ can be defined as "a learner of Jesus who accepts the teaching of his Master, not only in belief but in life-style." It involves acceptance of the views and practices of the Teacher and obedience to His commands.

When J. Edgar Hoover was head of the Federal Bureau of Investigation in Washington, he interviewed a young Communist who volunteered this statement: "We communists do not learn in order to show what a high IQ we have. *We learn in order to put into practice what we have learned."* That attitude is the essence of true discipleship.

The Communist Party requires of its members absolute commitment. One of their leaders asserted, "In Communism we have no spectators." Lenin went further and said that they would not accept into membership anyone with any reservation whatsoever. Only active, disciplined members of one of their organizations were eligible for membership.

When we respond to Christ's call to discipleship, we enter His school and place ourselves under His instruction. Originally "Christian" and "disciple" were interchangeable terms, but they cannot be so used today. Many who would wish to be classed as Christians are unwilling to comply with Christ's stringent conditions of discipleship.

Jesus never led His disciples to believe that the path of discipleship would be primrose-strewn. He coveted men and women who would follow Him through thick and thin. He was aiming more for quality than for quantity, so He did not tone down His requirements in order to gain more recruits.

In the course of His teaching ministry, Jesus enunciated three fundamental principles to guide His disciples in their service.

THE CONTINUANCE PRINCIPLE

"Jesus said to the Jews who had believed in him, '*If you continue in my word you are truly my disciples*, and you will know the truth and the truth will make you free'" (John 8:31-32, RSV*; italics added).

This gives us the *inward* view of discipleship, permanent continuance in the words of the Master, the attitude of scholar to teacher. Where that is absent, discipleship is nominal and lacks reality.

What is the significance of "my word" in the passage? In a sense it is indistinguishable from Himself, for He is the living Word. The sense here, however, is that of the whole tenor and substance of His teaching. It stands

* *Revised Standard Version.*

for His message as a whole, not favorite passages or pet doctrines but the whole range of His teaching.

His conversation with the two disciples on the Emmaus road is revealing in this connection: "Beginning with Moses and all the Prophets, he explained to them what was said in all the Scriptures concerning himself" (Luke 24:27).

To continue in His Word (or "to hold to his teaching," as the *New International Version* has it) was to make it their rule of life in daily practice. Our discipleship begins with the reception of the Word. Continuance in the Word is the evidence of reality.

Columba was an evangelist who left his native Ireland in A.D. 563 to bring the gospel to Scotland. He realized that he would face great difficulties and would be tempted to return home. A mound on the beach where he buried his boat when he landed was mute testimony to the reality of his purpose to obey the Lord's command to "make disciples of all nations." He committed himself to discipleship without any reservations.

At a conference in Ben Lippen, South Carolina, a young woman was giving testimony to her call to service. In the course of her message she held up a blank sheet of paper, saying that it contained God's plan for her life. The only writing on it was her signature at the bottom. Then she said, "I have accepted God's will without knowing what it is, and I am leaving it to Him to fill in the details." She was a true disciple, and she was on safe ground. With such a yielded will, the Holy Spirit would be able to guide her mental processes as she moved along the path of life.

Some decide to follow Christ on impulse, making their decision on the crest of a wave of enthusiasm that too often proves short-lived. It was with such a person in mind that our Lord stressed the importance of first counting the cost before making a decision with such far-reaching implications. An impulsive decision often lacks the element of intelligent commitment, with the result that when its implications become more clear, the cost proves too great and they fail to "continue in the word of Christ."

Others are willing to follow Christ—on a short-term basis. However, there is no such thing in the New Testament as short-term discipleship. The location in which our discipleship is exercised may be for only a short term, but total commitment is involved. The short-term disciple does not burn his bridges behind him, or bury his boat as Columba did. He never ventures as far as the point of no return.

A young man said to me: "I think I will take a trip to Asia and look around and try it out. If I feel comfortable about it, I might possibly return as a missionary." But in giving His Great Commission the Lord did not make the comfort of the messenger a deciding factor. One whose commitment was so desultory would be no asset to the missionary force.

That great Methodist preacher Samuel Chadwick stated the implications of discipleship in stark terms that recognize the lordship of Christ: "We are moved by the act of God. Omniscience holds no conference. Infinite authority leaves no room for compromise. Eternal love offers no explanations. The Lord expects to be trusted. He disturbs us at will. Human arrangements are disregarded, family ties ignored, business claims put aside. We are never asked if it is convenient."

Having said that, it should be noted that God is not only a sovereign Lord who can do as He wills, but also a loving Father whose paternity will never clash with His sovereignty. That reassuring truth is clearly stated in Isaiah's words: "Yet, O Lord, you are our Father. We are the clay, you are the potter" (Isaiah 64:8). The fatherhood of God is our guarantee that His sovereignty will never require of us anything that will not in the long run be in our highest interests (Hebrews 12:10). Continuance in Christ's Word is not automatic; it is the result of strong purpose and self-discipline. It demands taking time, not only to read the Scriptures but to meditate on them, turning them over in the mind in the same way the cow chews the cud. It will include memorization—hiding His Word in our hearts. Further, it will need to be "mixed with faith." Without that, our reading will bring little spiritual profit. Of the Hebrew Christians it was said, "The message they heard was of no value to them, because those who heard did not combine it with faith" (Hebrews 4:2).

There is a striking parallel and a vital connection between Colossians 3:16-25 and Ephesians 5:18–6:8. It will be noted that the same results that follow being filled with the Spirit (Ephesians 5:18) are attributed in Colossians to letting the word of Christ dwell in us richly (Colossians 3:16). Is not the obvious conclusion that these two are Siamese twins? We will remain filled with the Spirit just so long as we let the word of Christ dwell in us richly.

THE LOVE PRINCIPLE

"A new command I give you: Love one another. As I have loved you, so you must love one another. By this *all men will know that you are my disciples, if you love one another*" (John 13:34-35; italics added).

Those verses give the *outward* view of discipleship and have to do with our relations with our fellow men.

On Saturday evenings it was the custom in the home of the godly Samuel Rutherford to prepare for the Lord's Day by going through the catechism with his family. Question and answer went around the table.

One evening the exercise was interrupted by a knock at the door. The hospitable Rutherford invited the stranger to join the family circle. When it was the stranger's turn to answer, the question was, "How many commandments are there?"

"Eleven," he replied.

Rutherford was astonished that a so obviously well-educated man should be so ignorant, so he corrected him. The stranger, however, justified his answer by quoting the words of Jesus: "A new commandment I give you, that you love one another" (John 13:34; NASB*).

Rutherford extended hospitality to him for the night. As he was walking to the church on the morning of the Lord's Day, he heard a voice raised in prayer behind the hedge and recognized the voice of the stranger. It was a wonderful prayer, and the surprised minister waited until the stranger emerged.

"Who are you?" he inquired.

"I am Archbishop Ussher, the Primate of Ireland," was the reply. "I had heard so much about your piety," he continued, "that I took this method of finding out for myself."

As they talked, their hearts flowed together in their common devotion to the Lord. Not surprisingly the Archbishop was invited to preach, and you can guess his text: "A new commandment I give to you."

As we have seen, a disciple of Christ is one who not only studies His teaching but obeys His commands as well. In that instance the command is accompanied by example—"As I have loved you, so you must love one another" (John 13:34).

Aversion and affinity are alike irrelevant. We are to love our fellows, not because we like them or because they are attractive. Our love must not be selective—because of family or social ties, or because they are neighbors geographically—but simply because we are obligated to share the love of Christ with others.

* *New American Standard Bible.*

How did Jesus express His love? We are to express it in the same way.

His was *selfless love.* Even in the noblest human love there is usually some element of self-interest. We love, in part, because of what we receive from it—the happiness it brings. Our Lord's love was entirely disinterested and unselfish.

It was *forgiving love.* The only one who can forgive is the one against whom the offense has been committed. Although He was doubted, denied, betrayed, forsaken, the Lord's love was not quenched—"as I have loved you." When He told Peter that his forgiveness was to extend not to seven offenses but to seventy times seven, He was only illustrating the extent of His love for His failing disciples.

It was *sacrificial love.* In His earthly life Jesus gave Himself without stint. When He forgave the needy woman who crept up and touched the fringe of His garment, "at once Jesus realized that power had gone out from him" (Mark 5:30). His service was always at cost to Himself. There was no limit to the sacrifices He was prepared to make. It is the highest love that gives without any prospect of return.

The supreme evidence of discipleship, the authentic badge, is genuine love for one another. When people see it exemplified in shoe-leather, they will say, "These are true disciples of Christ. We can see it by the warmth of their love for one another." We can preach, pray, give, and even sacrifice, but without this love we gain nothing, are spiritual nonentities (1 Corinthians 13:2).

One writer remarks that the lesson Jesus taught was not only for advanced scholars. It is equally applicable to those in the kindergarten class. This love will be developed at first in private between scholar and Teacher, but it must soon become public evidence of discipleship.

THE FRUIT PRINCIPLE

"If you remain [continue] in me and my words remain in you, ask whatever you wish, and it will be given you. This is to my Father's glory, *that you bear much fruit, showing yourself to be my disciples*" (John 15:7-8; italics added).

This passage reveals the *upward* view of discipleship. A fruitless disciple of Christ is a contradiction in terms. If there is no real fruit in our lives, we cannot claim to be true disciples.

What constitutes the "fruit" of which the Lord spoke? Primarily the fruit is for God and His glory, and only secondarily for man. It is manifested in two areas.

Fruit in character—in the inward life. "The fruit of the Spirit is love, joy, peace, patience, kindness, goodness, faithfulness, gentleness and self-control" (Galatians 5:22-23).

The fruit of the Spirit's working in our lives is expressed in nine winsome graces. A tree is known by its fruit. The disciple is recognized by his likeness to Christ in inward character. It was to this end that Paul toiled. "I seek the fruit that increases to your credit" (Philippians 4:17, RSV).

Fruit in service—in outward ministry. "Open your eyes and look at the fields! They are ripe for harvest. Even now the reaper draws his wages, even now he harvests the crop for eternal life, so that sower and reaper may be glad together" (John 4:35-36). Fruit is seen when souls are won for Christ, discipled by concerned disciples, and led on to spiritual maturity.

The fruit-bearing that is an authentic mark of discipleship is not automatic but optional. Jesus made this clear when He said, "I tell you the truth, unless a kernel of wheat falls into the ground and dies, it remains only a single seed. But if it dies, it produces many seeds" (John 12:24). He thus links fruit-bearing with the cross. And did He not exemplify this principle in His own death? A single kernel of wheat fell into the ground at Calvary and died, but on the Day of Pentecost it produced three thousand kernels, and fruitage has resulted ever since.

The operative words in the statement in John 12 are "unless" and "if." The glorious possibility of "much fruit" lies in our own hands. "It is enough for the student to be like his teacher, and the servant like his master" (Matthew 10:25). It is as we apply the cross to our lives and die to the self-dominated life that the Spirit can make our lives fruitful.

4
TESTS OF DISCIPLESHIP

"I will follow you, Lord; but . . . " (Luke 9:61).

As our Lord was walking along the road on His way
to Jerusalem, He took the opportunity of giving His disciples a challenging insight into what was involved in following Him (Luke 9:57-62). He cited the cases of three
men, each of whom acknowledged His lordship and His
right of command. Each was a candidate for service, but
at the very outset of his candidacy, each found himself
faced with a stringent test of the reality of his discipleship.

In His reply to the first candidate, Jesus presented
the path of discipleship under the figure of plowing a
field, and a straight furrow from which there was to be
no deviation. Everyone who becomes a disciple of Christ,
by that action puts his hand to the plow; but there are
many influences to deflect him from turning a straight
furrow. Three of these emerge from this passage.

THE IMPULSIVE VOLUNTEER

"I will follow you wherever you go" (Luke 9:57). In a
burst of enthusiasm he made a voluntary and uncondi-
tional offer of service to the Lord. His sincerity was not
questioned. He was a volunteer prepared to go anywhere
after Jesus. Surely Jesus would warmly welcome this en-
thusiastic soul into His entourage.

But Jesus knew what was in men. John made this startling statement about His insight: "He knew men so well, all of them . . . he himself could tell what was in a man" (John 2:25, NEB*). He discerned that while this candidate was genuine, he was not yet ready for service.

He would have been a good "catch" for the Lord, for Matthew tells us he was a scribe (8:19, NASB); but Jesus saw in him a too fast follower. He saw that his enthusiasm would be likely to evaporate in times of testing.

The man would doubtless have expected to be welcomed with open arms by the new Teacher and would have been surprised at the Lord's cryptic and cautious response. Jesus had discerned a similarity between this man's response and Peter's protestation: "Even if all fall away on account of you, I never will" (Matthew 26:33).

A generous impulse ought not to be stifled, but Jesus saw in that volunteer one who had spoken without counting the cost involved. He did not reject his offer of service but made a cryptic statement that would open his eyes to the realities of the situation: "Foxes have holes and birds of the air have nests, but the Son of Man has no place to lay his head" (Luke 9:58).

In effect Jesus asked him, "Do you realize where your enthusiasm may lead you?" He was always transparently honest with would-be followers because He wanted their allegiance to be intelligent. So He sifted the man's motives as He sifts ours: "Take your time. Are you willing to face the sacrifices? Foxes and birds have their homes, but are you prepared to be homeless? Are you prepared to accept a lower standard of living for My sake?"

Bishop Ryle rightly maintained that nothing causes so much backsliding as enlisting disciples without letting them know what they are taking in hand. Such a charge could never be laid at Christ's door.

* *New English Bible.*

That was the test of poverty. The enthusiast must become the realist.

Although casualties are no less inevitable in spiritual warfare than in temporal military campaigns, it is not fair to send soldiers into battle without first briefing them on what is to be expected, and that is what Jesus was doing.

In these days of the welfare state, there is a growing demand for security against "the slings and arrows of outrageous fortune," and not every candidate for service is prepared to forgo this privilege. Before ever he embarks on missionary service, many a candidate displays an unhealthy interest in retirement benefits and holidays and working hours. Discipleship is a whole time job and a whole life job.

I recently received a letter that contained this challenging statement:

> Our modern emphases are so experience-orientated, and so centered on happiness and warm feelings instead of holiness and hard thinking, that some Christians' faith is nearer to the Buddhist's search for peace in the environment than to the message of the cross in history.

In the economic flux of our times we are learning painfully that there is no security in material things. They can be swept away overnight. The Lord offers us no security except in Himself. But is not that sufficient? Let us emulate adventurous Abraham who left the security of sophisticated Ur of the Chaldees and went out, "even though he did not know where he was going" (Hebrews 11:8). But though he had to tread an unknown path, he persevered because "he was looking forward to the city with foundations, whose architect and builder is God" (Hebrews 11:10). He had broken with the tyranny of the material.

There is indeed a cost in loyal discipleship, but there is also assurance of abundant compensation. It is impossible to out-give God. We may lose in material things but never in terms of joy and fulfillment here and eternal bliss hereafter.

THE RELUCTANT CONSCRIPT

"Lord, first let me go and bury my father" (Luke 9:59). The second candidate for service did not volunteer. He responded to the Lord's call "Follow me." But his response held a reservation. What he really meant was, "Let me attend to my home affairs first." If the first man was too fast, this candidate was too slow. To him, discipleship was a matter of only secondary importance.

Matthew informs us that the second man was already a follower of Jesus when he was called (8:21), so it is apparent that he was dragging his feet and putting other things before his commitment to Christ. True, he said in effect, "I will follow you," but he added an unacceptable rider—"when it suits my convenience." His devotion to Christ was casual, not vital. He was not ready to take the decisive step to burn all his bridges behind him. The Lord's cryptic reply was a challenge to do just that.

At first our Lord's reply seems rather harsh and unfeeling. Was it not natural and right for the man to attend his father's funeral? In Palestine it was required of elder sons to carry out the funeral ceremonies of their parents. He would have been adjudged unfilial if he did not do so. But there is another side to the story.

During a visit to the Holy Land, Sir George Adam Smith, a noted expositor, heard a man with whom he was traveling use exactly the same expression. On making inquiry he discovered that there was no literal funeral involved. His father was alive, but it was a colloquial saying in common use and really meant, "Let me attend to my family interests." Another traveler in the East heard a man use the same expression with his father sitting alongside him!

In His reply, "Let the dead bury their own dead, but you go and proclaim the kingdom of God" (Luke 9:60), Jesus implied that if he would put God's interests first, his family interests would not suffer. In any case, even if a literal funeral were involved, there would doubtless be other relatives who did not share his discipleship and were not concerned about the interests of the kingdom who would attend to the funeral arrangements. All other interests must come second if one is to be a true disciple. He must learn—and so must we—that where there is a clash of interests, Christ can be divisive.

God is not indifferent to family relationships and responsibilities. He does not speak with two voices, urging great care and compassion in those relations on the one hand and then making harsh, contrary demands on the other. But even home ties must come second to His requirements.

In setting out the conditions of discipleship in Luke 14, Jesus further clarified the issue: "If anyone comes to me and does not hate his father and mother, his wife and children, his brothers and sisters—yes, even his own life —*he cannot be my disciple*" (v. 26; italics added). When Christ is given unrivaled love and obedience, Jesus promised wonderful compensation; and no one would be the loser.

This can be much more than an academic problem in Christian service, especially in the realm of missions. The call of God comes to some disciples to leave home and preach the kingdom overseas. What of aged parents and other relatives left behind?

Where there is an absolute need and there are no other acceptable alternatives, the right course would be for the candidate to stay at home until the situation changes. Otherwise, despite the pull of natural affection, the course for the committed disciple is clear. "Go and proclaim the kingdom of God" (9:60). Unsympathetic or unspiritual relatives and friends may be critical, but our primary loyalty is to our Lord and Master.

In these days when there are so many unstable and broken marriages, there is in many churches a commendable emphasis on the importance of maintaining strong family ties. But even this good thing can get out of balance.

I recently talked with a family man who had attended seminars that rightly stressed the importance of parents spending quality time with their children. But he carried that exhortation to an unscriptural extreme. "I must give my whole time to my family," he said. "I am not going to any church meetings during the week, and I am not taking on any church responsibilities so that I can give time to my family." To such a man the Lord would be likely to give an answer similar to that given to the reluctant conscript.

If the first test of discipleship was that of poverty, the second is the test of urgency.

THE HALF-HEARTED VOLUNTEER

"I will follow you, Lord; but first let me go back and say good-by to my family" (Luke 9:61).

If the first candidate was too fast, and the second too slow, the third was too pliable. His limited commitment had a "but" in it, and like the response of his predecessor, it had an ominous "me first" sound as well. It was to him that the Lord gave the most solemn and heart-searching challenge of all: "No one who puts his hand to the plow and looks back is fit for service in the kingdom of God" (v. 62).

Christ's reply uncovered the nature of that man's problem: his heart was back at his home, not with his Master. Jesus saw that soon he would be looking back and then turning back. There is so much to deflect us from the path of full discipleship. Many like this man are

willing for a limited commitment, yet there is always a
"but" in their following.

Two fine and gifted young people had completed
their first term of missionary service and had showed
great promise. We had great hopes for them. As they left
for furlough, my colleague said to me, "I don't think we
will see them back again." I strongly disagreed with him,
for I had detected no such indication. I asked him why he
had formed that opinion. He replied in three words—
"She never unpacked." With greater discernment than
mine, he had detected signs that her heart had never
been weaned from home. They never returned.

Those who insist on putting earthly relationships
first are the ones most likely to be deflected. The third
disciple was yielding to the backward tug of earthly relationships. Our subtle adversary is very skilled in playing
upon our natural affections. The tense of the verb our
Lord used indicated not a single backward look but a developing habit—"keeps on looking back." And which of
us has not felt that backward pull?

Elisha's response to the call to follow Elijah affords
a striking contrast to the attitude of the reluctant
volunteer.

> So Elijah went from there and found Elisha. . . .
> He was plowing with twelve yoke of oxen, and he him-
> self was driving the twelfth pair. Elijah went up to him
> and threw his cloak around him. Elisha then left his
> oxen and ran after Elijah. "Let me kiss my father and
> mother good-by," he said, "and then I will come with
> you."
>
> "Go back," Elijah replied. "What have I done to
> you?" So Elisha left him and went back. He took his
> yoke of oxen and slaughtered them. He burned the
> plowing equipment to cook the meat and gave it to the
> people, and they ate. Then he set out to follow Elijah
> and became his attendant. (1 Kings 19:19-21)

In a literal sense he burned his bridges behind him. It is to such total commitment that our Lord is calling us. But like the early disciples, we are inclined to say, "This is a hard saying."

What this volunteer was proposing was a postponement of service. There are very many who say, "Oh, I am willing to go"—but they don't go. The backward pull is too strong. A growing affection for one who does not share the vision; ambition and the allurement of material prosperity; the easier path of comfort and indulgence rather than the rugged path of self-denial—these and many other considerations encourage the backward look.

The conflict can be agonizing. I had a conversation with a student at Cambridge University in England. The student had heard the call of God to missionary service, but he faced a difficult choice. His father, who owned a business with two thousand employees, wanted him to come into the business and in due course manage it. But there were features about it that would have prevented him from responding to the divine call. It was a moving experience to be with that young man as he wrestled with the problem and made a costly decision.

Jesus said in the plainest words: "No one who puts his hand to the plow and looks [keeps on looking] back is fit for service in the kingdom of God." Let us pray this prayer:

> Keep me from turning back!
> My hand is on the plow,
>   My faltering hand.
> The wilderness and solitary place,
> The lonely desert with its interspace,
>   Keep me from turning back.
>
> The handles of my plow
> With tears are wet,

The shares with rust are spoiled,
  And yet, and yet,
  My God, my God,
Keep me from turning back.
                   (Anonymous)

5
THE DISCIPLE'S MASTER

"Ye call me Master and Lord: and you say well; for so I am" (John 13:13, KJV*).

"Jesus Christ . . . is Lord of all" (Acts 10:36).

The question of authority is one of the burning issues of our times. It is challenged in every sphere—in family, church, school, and community. This revolt against constituted authority has been responsible for the disastrous breakdown in law enforcement, with a consequent upsurge in crime and violence.

Without some central authority, society will disintegrate into chaos and anarchy. Every ship must have a captain, every kingdom a king, and every home a head if they are to function aright.

If this is true of society in general, it is no less true in the kingdom of Mansoul, as Bunyan termed it—in the lives of individual men and women. The crucial question to answer is, "In whose hands does the final authority rest?" For the Christian there are only two alternatives. The authority rests in the Master's hands or in mine. Scripture leaves us in no doubt as to who should hold it—"[He] is Lord of all."

---

* King James Version.

LORDSHIP SALVATION

In recent times in evangelical circles there has developed strident debate around what has been termed "lordship salvation," a name that has been applied to the view that, for salvation, a person must believe in Christ as Savior and submit to His authority. Some, at the other end of the spectrum, go so far as to say that to invite an unsaved person to receive Jesus Christ as Savior and Lord is a perversion of the gospel, and is adding to the scriptural teaching about salvation. "All that is required for salvation is believing the gospel message," says Thomas L. Constable.

On either side are godly men whose love for the Lord is beyond question, and each view aims to preserve the purity of the gospel presentation in our day. There must, therefore, be mutual respect, but both positions cannot be right.

In my view, it is defective teaching to divorce the Saviorhood of Christ from His lordship. Salvation is not merely believing certain doctrinal facts; it is trusting in and embracing the divine Person who is Lord of the universe and who atoned for our sins.

To suggest that a person can exercise saving faith in Christ while knowingly rejecting His right to lordship over his life, seems a monstrous suggestion. In salvation we are not accepting Christ in His separate offices. To deliberately say, "I will receive Him as Savior, but I will leave the matter of lordship until later, and then decide whether or not I will bow to His will," seems an impossible position, and cannot be sustained by Scripture.

Having said that, I would concede that many have genuinely believed in Christ who, through inadequate teaching, were never confronted with Christ's claim to lordship, and therefore they have not knowingly rejected it. The proof of the reality of their regeneration would be that as soon as they learn of Christ's claim, they submit to His mastery.

Christ's call was not merely to believe in Him but to be His disciple, and that involves more than "making a decision" or believing certain doctrinal facts. A disciple is one who learns of Christ with the purpose of obeying what he or she learns. Jesus did not commission His disciples to go and make *believers* of all nations, but *disciples;* the terms are not synonymous, although there can be no salvation without believing (Matthew 28:20).

When Peter preached the first sermon to the Gentiles in the house of Cornelius, he said, "He is Lord of all." But Peter had not always recognized and bowed to His lordship. When, prior to that visit he saw a vision of a sheet being let down from heaven, containing all kinds of animals, reptiles, and birds, he heard a voice say, "Get up, Peter. Kill and eat."

"Surely not, Lord!" Peter replied. "I have never eaten anything impure or unclean" (Acts 10:13-14). He set his opinion against the Lord and received a well-deserved rebuke. If Christ were lord of his life, he could not have said, "Surely not," to Him. If he said, "Surely not," that was a negation of His lordship.

Have we not sometimes done what Peter did? When the Holy Spirit has prompted us to pray, to witness, to give, to break with some sin, to respond to a call to missionary or other service, have we said, in effect if not in words, "Surely not, Lord"?

When speaking to a large crowd, Jesus concluded His message with these challenging words: "Why do you call me, 'Lord, Lord,' and do not what I say?" (Luke 6:46). Acknowledging Christ's lordship is more than repeating the chorus "He is Lord, He is Lord."

Mahatma Mohandas Ghandi was a patriot and mystic. He sincerely admired Jesus as a man, but on one occasion he said, "I cannot accord to Christ a solitary throne, for I believe God has been incarnated again and again." He was willing to concede to Him equality with Buddha, Muhammad, Confucius, Zoroaster, and the rest, but not a unique and solitary throne. Yet that is exactly what He demands and deserves.

"O Lord, our God, other lords besides you have ruled over us," said Isaiah (26:13). Note that he did not say "instead of you," but "besides you." Israel did not want to entirely reject Jehovah, but they invited other gods to share their allegiance. But God will tolerate no rivals, no divided loyalty. No normal wife would be willing to share her husband's love with another woman, but that was what Israel had done.

The "other lords" take various forms. With some it may be business, with others sports, or money, or some avocation that takes the place that is due Christ. The danger is that these "other lords," though legitimate in themselves, may take an inordinate place in our time and affection and may eventually oust the real Lord.

Ideally the coronation of Christ as lord of the life should take place at conversion. When we present the gospel to a seeking soul, we should follow the example of the Lord and not conceal the cost of discipleship. Christ was scrupulously open and honest on this point. Unfortunately, that is not always done.

It is noteworthy that immediately on his conversion Paul realized what his only possible attitude should be toward Jesus. As soon as he got the answer to his question, "Who are you, Lord?" and realized that Jesus was indeed the Son of God, he asked a second question, "What shall I do, Lord?" (Acts 22:10). That was a clear, unequivocal submission to His lordship. His subsequent life proved that he never withdrew that allegiance. It should be remembered that in New Testament times a confession of Christ as Lord meant an irreversible change in public life. It needs to be clearly stated and strongly emphasized in our day that the Lord Jesus Christ has absolute and final authority over the whole church and every member of it in all details of daily life.

Seeing that our adversary the devil is always trying to seduce the disciple from following Christ, it is not surprising that some disciples do withdraw their allegiance. When Christ's teaching runs counter to their worldly and carnal desires, they take the reins of life back into their own hands.

But Christ will not reign over a divided kingdom. If there was a time when Christ was really crowned as king in your life, it is salutary to ask the question, "Is Christ still king of my life in daily practice?" Thank God that even if allegiance has been withdrawn, on confession of that sin we can renew that coronation, and He will graciously reassume the throne.

What Is Involved in Christ's Lordship?

Let us examine what submitting to Christ's lordship really means.

FULL SUBMISSION TO HIS AUTHORITY

"In your hearts set apart Christ as Lord" (1 Peter 3:15).

The verb is in the imperative, so it calls for a definite act of the will, by which we take our place at the feet of Christ in absolute surrender. Paul states that this was the objective of His death and resurrection: "For this very reason Christ died and returned to life, *so that He might be the Lord,* of both the dead and the living" (Romans 14:9; italics added).

In one of the Napoleonic wars, Lord Nelson defeated the French navy. The defeated admiral brought his flagship alongside Nelson's vessel and went aboard to make his surrender. He approached Nelson smilingly, with his sword swinging at his side. He held out his hand to the victor.

Nelson made no response to this gesture but said quietly, "Your sword first, sir." Laying down the sword was a visible token of surrender.

So, like Paul, we must lay down the sword of our rebellion and self-will. Henceforth His will becomes the law of our lives. Our consistent attitude will be: "Thy will be done [in me] as it is done in heaven." Submission means the complete surrender of our rights. That sounds a frightening prospect, but the experience of millions has proved that it is the path of unimagined blessing.

> Make me a captive, Lord,
> And then I shall be free,
> Force me to render up my sword
> And I shall conqueror be.
> (George Mathieson)

RECOGNITION OF HIS OWNERSHIP

"He is Lord of all" (Acts 10:36).

The word *Lord* here carries the idea of an owner who has control of all His possessions. Unless we recognize that fact in practice, Christ's reign over us is purely nominal. We are His by creation, and we are His by purchase. Now we are His by self-surrender. All that we have we hold as trustees, not as owners. But His gifts are to be enjoyed. God "richly provides us with everything for our enjoyment" (1 Timothy 6:17).

The story of Sir John Ramsden of Huddersfield, England, provides an interesting sidelight on this aspect of truth. I have checked the accuracy of the story with an old man from Huddersfield, who, when a boy, used to run messages for a Quaker and was rewarded with an orange and a penny.

When quite a young man Sir John saw that Huddersfield was destined from its location in Yorkshire to become a great industrial center. Property was certain to acquire a largely increased value in the near future. He therefore began quietly to purchase houses and lands, and in a few years he was possessor of the whole of the town, with the exception of a cottage and garden that belonged to a Quaker gentleman.

All the overtures of the real estate men having proved futile, Sir John Ramsden himself called upon the Quaker to see what he could accomplish by personal influence. The usual courtesies having passed between the knight and the Quaker, Sir John Ramsden said, "I presume you know the object of my visit."

"Yes," said the Quaker, "I have heard that thou hast bought the whole of Huddersfield with the exception of this cottage and garden, and I have been earnestly solicited by thy agents to sell this. But I do not want to sell. The cottage was built for my own convenience and suits me well. The garden, too, is laid out to suit my tastes. Why should I sell them?"

Sir John Ramsden said, "I am prepared to make you a very generous proposal. I will put a golden sovereign on every inch of ground covered by this cottage and garden, if you will sell." Sir John felt sure a proposal of such nature would not be in vain. So he inquired, "Will you sell?"

"No," said the Quaker with a mischievous twinkle in his eye. "Not unless thou'lt put them on edge." That was altogether out of the question, and somewhat chagrined the knight rose to leave. As he was going the Quaker said, "Remember, Sir John, that Huddersfield belongs to thee and to me."

Although the Quaker owned a very small part of the town, he could walk over all the rest of Sir John's town to reach the part that belonged to him.

In every life in which Christ's claims are recognized only in part, a similar situation arises. Satan can say to Him, "That disciple belongs to You and to me! He is a Christian worker, but I control part of his life." Where

Christ is not lord in practice, life becomes a battleground of conflicting interests.

"Why do you call me 'Lord, Lord,' and do not do what I say?" (Luke 6:46).

Obedience from the heart is the true and unmistakable evidence of the reality of Christ's lordship in our lives. Disobedience vitiates all our professions of loyalty. Our performance speaks more loudly than our professions. The test is not what I say but what I do.

Were it not for Calvary's revelation of the heart of God, we might well fear God's sovereignty and think His demands tyrannical. Calvary has set that fear to rest once for all.

There was a man in Germany, a village organist, who one day was practicing on the church organ, playing a piece by that master of music Mendelssohn.

He was not playing it very well, and a stranger stole into the church and sat in the dimness of a back pew. He noted the imperfections of the organist's performance, and when the latter had ceased playing and was preparing to depart, the stranger made bold to go to him and say, "Sir, would you allow me to play for a little?"

The man said gruffly, "Certainly not! I never allow anybody to touch the organ but myself."

"I should be so glad if you would allow me the privilege!"

Again the man made a gruff refusal. The third time the appeal was allowed, but most ungraciously.

The stranger sat down, pulled out the stops, and on that same instrument began to play. And, oh, what a difference! He played the same piece, but with wonderful change. It was as if the whole church was filled with heavenly music.

The organist asked, "Who *are* you?"

In modesty the stranger replied, "My name is Mendelssohn."

"What!" said the man, now covered with mortification. "Did I refuse *you* permission to play on my organ?"

Let us not withhold any part of our lives from the mastery of Christ.

It may be that you are thinking, *I recognize Christ's claim to lordship of my life, and I want to live under His lordship, but my will is so weak. It lets me down at the crucial moment. How can I maintain recognition of His lordship? How can I keep Him on the throne of my life?*

Paul anticipated this dilemma when he wrote, "No one can say ("keep on saying" gives the tense of the verb) 'Jesus is Lord,' *except by the Holy Spirit"* (1 Corinthians 12:3; italics added).

The Holy Spirit is sent to enable the disciple to keep Christ on the throne of the believer's life, and He delights to do it. He will detach our hearts from the world and attach our affections to Christ. He will empower our weak wills and make them strong to do the will of God.

> Other lords have long held sway,
> Now Thy name alone to hear,
> Thy dear voice alone obey,
> Is my daily, hourly prayer
> Let my heart be all Thine own,
> Let me live to Thee alone.
> (F. R. Havergal)

6

THE DISCIPLE'S
SENIOR PARTNER

"May the grace of the Lord Jesus Christ, and the love of God, and the fellowship [partnership] of the Holy Spirit be with you all" (2 Corinthians 13:14).

When a merchant is operating an expanding business venture, he is sometimes hampered in its development by a lack of capital. So he inserts an advertisement in the newspaper: "WANTED, a partner with capital, to join in developing a promising business."

The business of living the Christian life as it should be lived is too lofty in its ideals and too exacting in its demands for us to engage in it alone. We desperately need a partner with adequate capital to make it a success.

Certain statements of Scripture bring us face to face with the paucity of our spiritual capital. They make demands that are patently impossible for the unaided human nature. Verses such as those that follow, far from encouraging us, tend to fill us with dismay when we review our past performance.

"Be perfect, therefore, as your heavenly Father is perfect" (Matthew 5:48).

"It is written, Be ye holy; for I am holy" (1 Peter 1:16, KJV).

"Always giving thanks to God the Father for everything" (Ephesians 5:20).

"Do not be anxious about anything" (Philippians 4:6).

"Pray without ceasing" (1 Thessalonians 5:17, KJV).

What an impossible standard! How could ordinary men and women hope to reach such heights of spiritual attainment? "I can understand Paul getting high grades, but I'm no Paul!"

But is God so unreasonable as to make impossible demands and then hold us responsible for our failure? Our conscious spiritual inadequacy underlines our need of a partner who has adequate spiritual resources on which we can draw.

Here, as everywhere else, our bounteous God has anticipated our need and meets it through the operations of His Holy Spirit. That provision is implicit in the familiar benediction: "The fellowship of the Holy Spirit be with you all" (2 Corinthians 13:14).

The Greek word for "fellowship" is the familiar word that has recently come into common use in religious circles, *koinonia*. It is defined as meaning "partnership, participation in what is derived from the Holy Spirit."

Without straining the text, that is the staggering suggestion that the third Person of the Trinity is willing to become the active, though secret, Partner of the disciple in his walk and witness.

Five times in the New Testament *koinonia* is translated as "partner." It is used of a partnership in a fishing business: "They signaled their partners in the other boat to come and help them" (Luke 5:7). Thus "the partnership of the Holy Spirit" is a concept that is textually and etymologically supported.

THE PERSONALITY OF THE PARTNER

Most who read these pages will believe in the doctrine of the personality of the Holy Spirit—that He is not a mere power or influence that we can use for our purposes, but a divine Person. We believe the doctrine, but do we always recognize and honor Him as such in daily life? It is so easy to forget Him or to ignore Him unconsciously, and yet He is active in every aspect of life.

When Jesus was breaking the news of His approaching departure and the consequent coming of the Comforter to His disciples, He uttered four pregnant words that call for a searching of our hearts. He had already said: "If you really knew me, you would know my Father as well" (John 14:7). Then He added:

> If you love me, you will obey what I command. And I will ask the Father, and He will give you another Counselor to be with you forever—the Spirit of truth. The world cannot accept him because it neither sees him nor knows him. *But you know him,* for he lives with you and will be in you. (John 14:15-17; italics added)

In those passages Jesus speaks of our knowing Him, knowing the Father, and knowing the Holy Spirit. The Father concept in reference to the Godhead is familiar to us because we have fathers (although some fathers may be far from ideal). But we can conceive of God as a perfect Father. We *know* God as our Father.

Similarly, it is not too difficult for us to form a concept of Jesus as the Son of God, for He came to earth and revealed Himself as the Son of Man and fully identified Himself with our humanity, even to the extent of assuming our sinless weaknesses. We know Jesus as our Savior and Lord.

But can we say with equal definiteness that we *know* Him, the Holy Spirit, as a divine Person who is worthy of equal love and reverence with the Father and the Son? Do we enjoy His personal help and empowering in daily life, or is He just a mystical, shadowy figure of whom we have no clear concept?

It is helpful in this connection to consider the significance of the words "another Counselor" or Comforter. In Greek two words mean "another." One means "another of a different kind"; the other, "another of exactly the same kind." It is the second that Jesus used. He was assuring His disciples that His personal Representative whom He was sending was exactly like Himself. This Representative would be just as loving, tender, and caring—so much so that there would be an advantage to them in His own departure (John 16:7). Does that not dispel some of the shadow that tends to shroud His real personality? *He is exactly like Jesus.*

Since He is willing to be Partner with us in daily life, should we not get to know Him better?

The Purpose of the Partnership

If an earthly partnership is to be successful, it is of prime importance that there be a warm and trustful relationship between the partners. Also, if friction is to be obviated, they must be one in both aims and ideals.

I was once appointed executor of an estate that involved a business partnership. The surviving partners, although upright in character, held entirely opposing views of the direction the business should take. Ultimately, the dissension became so acute that the only course possible was to dissolve the partnership and sell the business. For success, there must be mutual trust and confidence and unity of aim.

The Holy Spirit has been sent to transact big business for the kingdom of God, nothing less than to participate in the redemption of a lost world. In this vast enterprise He seeks our partnership as He oversees the interests of Christ on earth.

Jesus spelled out the Spirit's primary ministry in six words: "He will bring glory to me" (John 16:14). Just as Christ's aim was to glorify His Father (John 17:4), so the aim of the Holy Spirit is to glorify Christ. If we are truly partners with the Spirit, then that will be our consuming objective too. So long as our genuine ambition is to glorify Christ, we can count on the aid of our Senior Partner, whether in home, school, office, or pulpit.

THE POSITION OF THE PARTNERS

Some businesses operate quite successfully with one member being a working partner and the other being a sleeping partner. The latter, though not involved in the day-to-day conduct of the business, makes an essential contribution by providing the capital for the operation. He, of course, shares proportionately in the profits.

The Holy Spirit, however, will not consent to be a sleeping partner, although He may be a secret Partner in the sense that He is not visible in the partnership business. He must be accorded the role of Senior Partner and have control of the whole enterprise if there is to be a harmonious and successful operation.

Could not many of our failures be attributed to the fact that we arrogate to ourselves the role of senior partner instead of ceding it to Him? Have we been guilty of trying to make use of Him instead of allowing Him to make use of us?

The story of Gideon illustrates this point. He became a powerful instrument in God's hands because he recognized correctly the relative positions of the Holy Spirit and himself: "Then the Spirit of the Lord came upon [clothed himself with] Gideon" (Judges 6:34).

Gideon's personality voluntarily became a garment, so to speak, in which God could move among men. He was thus enabled, through Gideon, to achieve a notable victory on behalf of His people.

When Dwight L. Moody and his wife were vacationing beside the Syrian Sea, an old man greatly amazed Moody by saying, "Young man, honor the Holy Spirit or thou shalt break down."

"I was angry," Moody said, "but he was right. I was troubled, and prayed until there came a night when Third Heaven found me. Since then my soul has known the mystery of Moses' burning bush which burned with fire, but was not consumed."

If in our service we honor the Holy Spirit, and consistently respect His position as Senior Partner, we will not be prone to suffer from the contemporary malady of "burnout." We will not be undertaking work for God in our own strength or embarking on enterprises He has not initiated. The last word in any decision must lie with the Senior Partner.

PARTICULARS OF THE PARTNERSHIP

If a partnership is to run harmoniously, the terms of partnership must be clearly understood and set out in writing, down to the last particular. It is unwise to enter into a partnership arrangement, even though it be with friends, without a signed and sealed deed of partnership setting out the mutual privileges and responsibilities of the partners.

What does Scripture have to say about the terms on which the Holy Spirit will be able to work with us? I will suggest five that usually have their counterpart in a human partnership agreement:

The business shall be conducted according to the partnership agreement. The Spirit-breathed Word of God is, of course, our deed of partnership. No contingency can arise in our work for the kingdom for which provision has not been made there. Our first duty is to acquaint ourselves with those provisions and conform our lives to their demands.

The partners shall devote their whole time, abilities, and energies to furthering the partnership business. There is no question of the Holy Spirit's failing to honor His obligations. The risen Lord assured us of His cooperation and empowering: "You will receive power when the Holy Spirit comes on you, and you will be my witnesses" (Acts 1:8).

Like his Lord, the disciple should be willing to subordinate personal interests and comforts to the concerns of the kingdom. He should not enter into secret alliances with competitors or others whose interests are adverse —the world, the flesh, or the devil.

The capital to be contributed by each partner. It is at this point we come face to face with our spiritual bankruptcy. What have we got to contribute? James M. Gray states our position in verse:

> Naught have I gotten but what I received,
> Grace has bestowed it since I have believed.
> Once more to tell it would I embrace,
> I'm only a sinner, saved by grace.

My only contribution to the partnership assets is my redeemed personality with its powers and possibilities. Because I was made "in the image of God," I am acceptable to my Partner despite my penury. So I present my contribution:

> All for Jesus, all for Jesus,
> All my being's ransomed powers,
> All my thoughts, and words and actions,
> All my days, and all my hours.

But what will the Holy Spirit contribute? He has been authorized to make "the unsearchable riches of Christ" available to us (Ephesians 3:8). "All the treasures of wisdom and knowledge" are part of the capital (Colossians 2:3). Why do we not appropriate more of what has been given to equip us for effective service?

A young man was suddenly launched into a business that expanded rapidly. He was quite unknown in business circles, and he himself had very little capital. Yet he did not appear to be financially embarrassed. What they did not know was that an anonymous wealthy man, discerning the capabilities of the young man, had said to him, "You begin a business, and I will stand by you financially." The mystery was solved. It is in this sense that the Holy Spirit is our divine Standby.

In the event of any disagreement or dispute arising, the matter shall be referred to an arbitrator. Who is the arbitrator if I fail to fulfill the terms of the partnership agreement? If the dove of peace has flown from my heart, that will be evidence that I am out of harmony with my Senior Partner; I will have grieved the Holy Spirit. An honest confession of sin and failure and a renewal of obedience will secure the return of the dove of peace. One rendering of Philippians 4:7 has it: "May the peace of God be enthroned in your heart as the arbitrator in all disputes."

The distribution of profits. In our association with the Holy Spirit, we are given the best of the bargain all the way through. Unlike other partners, He seeks nothing for Himself. In spite of our negligible contribution to the capital, He makes all the profits over to us, and we are constituted "heirs of God and co-heirs with Christ" (Romans 8:17).

THE PRIVILEGES OF THE PARTNERSHIP

What abundant benefits accrue to us through our association with our Lord's Representative on earth!

In Bible study. The Spirit of truth is both inspirer and interpreter of the Scriptures. He illumines the sacred page as we traverse it under His guidance. He delights to unfold before our eyes the glories, virtues, and achievements of the Savior. He imparts "the light of the knowledge of the glory of God in the face of Christ" (2 Corinthians 4:6).

In the prayer life. He is called the "spirit of grace and supplication" (Zechariah 12:10), and in this role He "helps us in our weakness [for] we do not know what we ought to pray for" (Romans 8:26). Much of the barrenness of our prayer lives can be attributed to our failure to appropriate the promised help of our Partner.

In our service. We can draw upon His mighty power to enable us to do everything that is within the scope of the will of God. The risen Christ promised this equipment: "You will receive power when the Holy Spirit comes on you" (Acts 1:8).

In our character. The passion of the Holy Spirit is to transform us into the likeness of Christ, as Paul intimates:

> And we who with unveiled faces all reflect [behold] the Lord's glory, are being transformed into his likeness with ever-increasing glory, which comes from the Lord, who is the Spirit. (2 Corinthians 3:18)

With that light on the all too familiar benediction, it should have much more meaning for us.

7

THE DISCIPLE'S SERVANTHOOD

"I am among you as one who serves" (Luke 22:27).

"No servant is greater than his master" (John 15:20).

In Isaiah's prophecy, the phrase "servant of the Lord" is used in three distinct senses. It is used of the nation of Israel: "But you, O Israel, my servant, Jacob, whom I have chosen. . . . I said, 'You are my servant'" (41:8-9).

It is used of the children of God: "This is the heritage of the servants of the Lord, and this is their vindication from me, declares the Lord" (54:17).

It is used anticipatively of the Messiah, Christ: "Here is my servant, whom I uphold, my chosen one in whom I delight" (42:1).

God selected Israel from among the nations to represent Him on earth and to be a light among the godless nations of the world, but they failed Him at every turn. Christ, the promised Messiah, rendered the perfect devotion and service that Israel had failed to give and met the highest ideals of both His Father and of man. In chapter 42:1-4, a messianic passage, Isaiah depicts the ideal Servant of Jehovah and the qualities He will display.

In the incident when Jesus washed His disciples' feet as servant, He said to them, "I have set you an example that you should do as I have done for you. . . . No servant is greater than his master." (John 13:15-16). His attitude is the pattern for the disciple. Only twice in Scripture is Christ specifically stated to be our example: once in connection with service, and, significantly, the other in connection with suffering (1 Peter 2:21).

The supreme revelation of lowly service recorded in John 13 was no new office for our Lord, for He is "the same yesterday and today and forever" (Hebrews 13:8). He was only manifesting in time what He had always been in eternity. On that occasion He acted out the master principle of service—that the highest honor lies in the lowliest service. He revealed to us that the life of God is spent in the service of humanity. There is no one so perpetually available as He. He rules all because He serves all.

Jesus was no revolutionary in the political sense, but in no area was His teaching more revolutionary than in that of spiritual leadership. In the contemporary world the term *servant* has a lowly connotation, but Jesus equated it with greatness: "Whoever wants to become great among you must be your servant, and whoever wants to be first must be slave of all" (Mark 10:43-44).

Most of us would have no objection to being a master or a mistress, but servanthood and slavery have little attraction. And yet that is the way the Master went. He knew that such an other worldly concept would not be welcomed by an indulgent and ease-loving world of men. But He did not reduce His standards to attract disciples.

It should be noted that in stating the primacy of servanthood in His kingdom, He did not have in mind mere acts of service, for those can be performed from very dubious motives. He meant the spirit of servanthood.

Principles of the Lord's life that are to be reproduced in the lives of those of us who are His disciples include:

Dependence

"Here is my servant, whom I uphold" (Isaiah 42:1).

That is one of the amazing aspects of the self-emptying of Christ in His incarnation. In becoming man, Jesus did not divest Himself of any of His divine attributes or prerogatives, but He did empty Himself of self-will and self-sufficiency. Although He was "upholding all things by the word of his power" (Hebrews 1:3, KJV), so closely did He identify Himself with us in all the sinless infirmities of human nature that He too needed the divine upholding. His own words testify to this: "I tell you the truth, the Son can do nothing by himself" (John 5:19); "My teaching is not my own. It comes from him who sent me" (John 7:16); "These words you hear are not my own; they belong to the Father who sent me" (John 14:24).

Taken together, those verses indicate that Jesus chose to be dependent on His Father for both His words and His works. Are we as dependent as He was? This divine paradox is one of the amazing aspects of His incarnation, when He took "the very nature of a servant" (Philippians 2:7). The Holy Spirit will be able to use us to the measure that we adopt the same attitude. The danger is in our being too independent.

Acceptance

"My chosen one in whom I delight" (Isaiah 42:1).

Although the Father met with little more than disappointment with His servant Israel, He found delight in the attitudes and achievements of His Son. On two occasions He broke the silence of eternity to declare His pleasure in Him. Christ was a servant who never failed to shed abroad the fragrance of a self-forgetful ministry. It rose to heaven as an aromatic cloud. We too are God's chosen ones, "accepted in Him."

SELF-EFFACEMENT

"He will not shout or cry out, or raise his voice in the streets" (v. 2).

One rendering is, "He will not be loud and screamy." The ministry of God's servant would not be strident and flamboyant but modest and self-effacing. That is a most desirable quality in a day of blatant self-advertisement, of TV brashness and mounting decibels.

The devil tempted Jesus on this point when he challenged Him to create a stir by jumping from the parapet of the Temple. But He did not fall into the tempter's snare. On the contrary, He silenced those who would blazon His miracles abroad. Often He stole away from the adulation of the crowd. He performed no miracle to enhance His own prestige.

It is recorded of the cherubim, those angelic servants of the Lord, that they used four of their six wings to conceal their faces and feet—a graphic representation of contentment with hidden service.

EMPATHY

"A bruised reed he will not break, and a smoldering wick he will not snuff out" (v. 3).

The weak and erring, the failures, are often crushed under the callous tread of their fellow men. But the ideal Servant specializes in ministry to those who are generally despised or ignored. No life is so bruised and broken that He will not restore it.

Ambitious and self-seeking Christian workers, like the priest and the Levite, pass by on the other side of the street in order to devote themselves to a higher stratum of society. They are not willing to keep teaching the elements of the gospel to simple believers, or to endeavor to encourage backsliders onto the narrow way. They want a ministry more worthy of their powers.

Jesus, however, found delight and satisfaction in stooping to serve those whom most choose to ignore. His skillful, loving care caused the broken reed once again to produce heavenly music and fanned the dimly burning wick into a glowing flame. He never entirely crushed or condemned the penitent. It is noble work to care for those whom the world ignores.

How dimly Peter's wick burned in Pilate's judgment hall! But what a brilliant flame blazed on the day of Pentecost. The Master Himself fanned the spark so effectually in that private interview that it kindled the Pentecost conflagration.

E. Stanley Jones said, "Jesus was patient with and hopeful for the weak and faltering and sinful. And yet He did not compromise and accommodate Himself to their imperfections and sins. He held them to victory and not to defeat."

Optimism

"He will not falter or be discouraged till he establishes justice on earth" (v. 4).

The *Revised Standard Version* has it, "He will not be disheartened or crushed." A pessimist will never be an inspiring leader. We will look in vain for pessimism in the life or ministry of the pattern Servant. He was a realist but not a pessimist. He evinced an unshakable confidence in the fulfillment of His Father's purposes and in the coming of the kingdom.

It is not by accident that the words "falter" and "discouraged" in verse 4 are the same in the original as "break" and "quench" in verse 3. The implication is that though God's Servant engages in a gracious ministry to bruised reeds and smoking wicks, He is neither one nor the other. The essential elements of hope and optimism will be justified by the achievement of His objective.

Anointing

"Here is my servant . . . I will put my Spirit on him" (v. 1).

By themselves the five preceding qualities will be insufficient equipment for divine service. In truth the disciple needs a touch of the supernatural. That was supplied for God's ideal Servant in the anointing of the Spirit. "God anointed Jesus of Nazareth with the Holy Spirit and power . . . he went around doing good and healing all who were under the power of the devil" (Acts 10:38).

All that He did was through the empowering of the Holy Spirit. Until the Spirit descended on Him at His baptism, He created no stir in Nazareth; then world-shaking events began to happen.

The same Spirit and the same anointing is available to us. We should not attempt what our divine Exemplar would not do—embark upon ministry without being anointed by the Spirit.

God does not give the Spirit by measure (John 3:34). It is only our capacity to receive that regulates the supply of the Spirit (Philippians 1:9). What happened to our Lord at Jordan, and to the 120 when "they were all filled with the Spirit" on the Day of Pentecost, must happen to us if we are to fulfill God's ideal for us as His servants.

Ministries of the Servant

The disciple is called to be both a minister and a priest: "You will be called priests of the Lord, you will be named ministers of our God" (Isaiah 61:6).

The priests ministered to the Lord. The Levites ministered to their brethren. It is the privilege of the disciple to minister to both, and we must therefore keep in balance the worship of God and service to man.

We are to offer spiritual sacrifices in the sanctuary and to engage in the other duties of the house of God as well.

The Servant is responsible to mediate the light of the gospel, as a light to the nations, and rescue the captives from the prison house of sin (Isaiah 42:6-7). But His supreme responsibility is to glorify God. "You are my servant, Israel, in whom I will display my splendor" (Isaiah 49:3).

In reviewing His earthly life, the ideal Servant summarized the whole in one sentence, which is for our emulation: "I have brought you glory on earth by completing the work you gave me to do" (John 17:4).

8

THE DISCIPLE'S AMBITION

"So whether I am at home or away from home, it is my constant ambition to please him" (2 Corinthians 5:9, Williams).

It is the responsibility of the disciple to be the best he or she can be for God. To please Him is a most worthy aim. He wants us to realize the full purpose of our creation; He does not want us to be content with bland mediocrity. Many fail to achieve anything significant for God or man because they lack a dominating ambition. No great task was ever achieved without the complete abandonment to it that a worthy ambition inspires.

Fred Mitchell was a pharmacist before he became the British Director of the China Inland Mission. He told me that when he was a student, he and a friend took a course in optometry. One day the latter made a startling statement that bordered on the realm of fantasy.

"One day I am going to be King George's optometrist," he said.

With predictable skepticism Fred replied, "Oh, yes?"

Fred then asked me, "Do you know who is the King's optometrist today? That same young man." He was in the grip of a master ambition that channeled his life in a single direction, and he reached his goal.

We would do well to ask ourselves if *we* have any such clearly defined ambition. Are we making the most of our lives? Are we exercising our maximum influence for our Lord?

THE PLACE OF AMBITION

Our English word *ambition* is not a New Testament word. It is derived from the Latin and has the doubtful distinction of meaning "facing both ways to gain an objective." A modern illustration of this word would be the electioneering tactics of an unprincipled and ambivalent politician canvassing for votes.

Worldly ambition can have a variety of ingredients, but it usually follows three main lines: *popularity*, fame, the desire to build a reputation; *power*, the desire to wield authority over one's fellows; *wealth*, the desire to amass a fortune, with the power that brings. The fatal flaw with such ambitions is that they all focus on *self*.

Even secular writers have seen the seamy side of such ambition, which has justifiably been termed "the last infirmity of noble minds." With his uncanny insight into the heart of man, Shakespeare put these words into the mouth of Cardinal Wolsey: "Cromwell, I charge thee, fling away ambitions. By that sin fell the angels, how can man then, the image of his Maker, hope to profit by it?"

But not all ambitions warrant these strictures. Paul employed a word that had a nobler ancestry and could be rendered "a love of honor." So 2 Corinthians 5:9 could be rendered, "So we make it a point of honor to please him."

Further, Paul asserts that "to aspire to leadership is an honorable ambition" (1 Timothy 3:1, NEB). Of course in this connection the motivation would be the determining factor. Too many disciples are content with the status quo and cherish no ambition to improve their spiritual condition and fulfill a more useful ministry.

At the Lord's command Jeremiah communicated to Baruch the divine exhortation: "Should you then seek great things *for yourself?* Seek them not" (Jeremiah 45:5; italics added). This injunction was not a blanket prohibition of ambition. The operative words are "for thyself." Baruch was counseled to abjure self-centered ambition. Jesus made clear that an ambition to be great is not in itself necessarily sinful (Mark 10:43). It was ambition to be great from unworthy motives that He denigrated. God needs great people whose dominant ambition is to further the glory of God.

THE TEST OF AMBITION

James and John were both ambitious men, but their ambition was almost entirely self-centered and therefore unworthy. Their ambition peeps out of their request of the Lord. "Let one of us sit at your right and the other at your left in your glory" (Mark 10:37). They actually asked Him to reserve the best seats for them in His coming kingdom! It was pure, unadulterated selfishness and warranted the rebuke it received: "Not so with you" (v. 43). The kingdom of God is founded on self-sacrifice, not on selfishness. James and John asked for a crown of glory; Jesus chose a crown of thorns. They wanted to rule over their fellows; He told them that the road to greatness was by serving, not by ruling. This is a tremendously important lesson for the disciple to master.

The ambition of Count Nikolaus Zinzendorf, founder of the great missionary Moravian church, was enshrined in these words: "I have one passion: it is He, He alone!" This Christ-centered passion and ambition was imprinted on the church he led. It pioneered a world missions program in a day when missionaries were few. For a hundred years there arose night and day an unbroken stream of prayer from the church at Herrnhutt. His was a worthy ambition that found its center in Christ and reached the world.

We can test the quality of our own ambition with this measuring stick: "Will the fulfillment of my ambition bring glory to God and make me more useful to Him in reaching out to a lost world?"

A MASTER AMBITION

David Brainerd, early missionary to the Indians of the United States, was so consumed with a passion for the glory of Christ in the salvation of souls that he claimed: "I cared not how or where I lived, or what hardships I endured, so that I could but gain souls for Christ."

Paul was a passionately ambitious man, even before his conversion. He could do nothing by halves. "I was exceedingly zealous," he declared. Always impatient of the confining status quo, he constantly strained toward new goals and horizons. There was in him a compulsion that would brook no denial.

His conversion did not quench the flame of his zeal but rather caused it to leap higher. Whereas his old ambition had been to efface the name of Jesus and exterminate His church, now he had a passion to exalt the name of Jesus and establish and edify His church. His new ambition found its center in the glory of Christ and the advancement of His kingdom.

In later life Paul wrote:

> It has always been my ambition to preach the gospel where Christ was not known, so that I would not be building on someone else's foundation. Rather, as it is written: "Those who were not told about him will see, and those who have not heard will understand." (Romans 15:20-21)

One writer suggested that Paul suffered from spiritual claustrophobia. His early commission had been to "Go . . . far away to the Gentiles" (Acts 22:21), and he was ambitious to discharge that trust. He was haunted by the "regions beyond," and every true disciple should share that ambition.

Henry Martyn, brilliant scholar and gallant missionary, expressed his master ambition in these words: "I desire not to burn out for avarice, to burn out for ambition, to burn out for self, but looking up at that great Burnt-offering, to burn out for God and His world."

Paul's ambition was fired by two powerful motives. First was the love of Christ, which "compelled" him, left him no option (2 Corinthians 5:14). That was the love that had captured and broken his rebellious heart. Second was a sense of inescapable obligation. "I feel myself under a sort of universal obligation," he said. "I owe something to all men, from cultured Greek to ignorant savage" (Romans 1:14, Phillips). Since all men were included in the scope of Christ's salvation, he felt equally indebted to all classes. Social status, poverty, illiteracy were alike irrelevant to him. His ambition was funneled into a single channel—"this one thing I do"—and it unified his whole life.

It is small wonder he succeeded in the face of daunting difficulties when he was so willing to pay the price of spiritual excellence. In his great poem "St. Paul," F. W. H. Myers highlights this:

> How have I knelt with arms of my aspiring,
> Lifted all night in irresponsive air,
> Dazed and amazed with overmuch desiring,
> Blank with the utter agony of prayer.

At the funeral of Dawson Trotman, founder of the wide-spreading Navigator movement, Billy Graham delivered the sermon. In the course of his address he made this revealing statement: "Here was a man who did not say, 'These forty things I dabble in,' but, 'This one thing I do.'" A master ambition such as that overcomes all obstacles and thrives on difficulties and discouragements.

Our Lord was gripped by a master ambition that integrated the whole of His life. It can be summarized in a single sentence: "I have come to do your will, O God" (Hebrews 10:7). When at life's end He offered His wonderful high-priestly prayer, He was able to report the complete achievement of this ambition: "I have brought you glory on earth by completing the work you gave me to do" (John 17:4).

CONTESTED AMBITION

As with the Master, so the ambition of the disciple will be challenged all along the way. There was so much to weaken His resolve and deflect Him from His purpose—the malignity of His enemies, the fickleness of His friends, and even the attempted dissuasion of His intimates.

Through years of mounting disappointments, Joseph maintained his integrity and loyalty to his God. One day in the course of his duties, he was seduced by his master Potiphar's wife. His godly purpose to keep himself pure stood him in good stead in the first shock of the unexpected temptation. But it was a constantly repeated assault: "Though she spoke to Joseph day after day, he refused to go to bed with her or even be with her" (Genesis 39:10). His purpose was challenged every day. The devil is a persistent tempter.

A study of the lives of men and women who have achieved great things for Christ and His church reveals that they have this in common: they cherished a master ambition.

Jonathan Edwards, noted revivalist and educator, declared: "I will live with all my life while I live."

The founder of the Salvation Army, William Booth, claimed: "So far as I know, God has had all there was of me."

With all the resources of God at our disposal, we need not plead our weakness or inadequacy as an excuse for poor performance. The least promising among us may yet be used greatly by God.

Thomas Scott, 1747-1821, was the dunce of his school. The teachers expected little of him, so why bother with him? But his brain and heart only needed to be awakened. One day some statement of a teacher penetrated his deepest being.

Then and there he formed a resolute purpose, a master ambition. Although his progress was slow, the teachers noticed a difference. He grew to be a strong and worthy man and succeeded the noted former slave-trader John Newton, composer of the hymn "Amazing Grace," as rector of the church at Aston Sandford. He also wrote a large and valuable commentary on the whole Bible, which had a great influence on his generation. So valuable was the work of this erstwhile dunce that the commentary is still available in America today.

Other class members are all forgotten. The one of whom least was expected, and who labored under the greatest handicap, is the one whose name and influence endures. And all because he was gripped by a master ambition.

In an article in *Crusade* magazine, John R. W. Stott has this to say about the lack of worthy ambition in our day:

> The motto of our generation is, "Safety first." Many young men are looking for a safe job in which they can feather their nest, secure their future, insure their lives, reduce all risks, and retire on a fat pension.
>
> There is nothing wrong in providing for your future, but this spirit pervades our lives until life becomes soft and padded and all adventure is gone. We are so thickly wrapped in cotton wool that we can neither feel the pain of the world nor hear the Word of God. . . .
>
> Jesus did not remain in the social immunity of heaven, or hide away in the safety of the skies. He en-

tered the zone of danger, risking contamination. . . . How can we make safety our ambition?

If we embrace Paul's ambition "to please Him," we will discover that at the same time we are pleasing everyone else who is worth pleasing.

9
THE DISCIPLE'S LOVE

"An alabaster jar of very expensive perfume. . . . It could have been sold for more than a year's wages" (Mark 14:3, 5).

The incident recounted in Mark 14:1-9, in which a woman broke a jar of expensive perfume and poured it on Jesus' head, is a glowing example of the extravagance of love. The context of the action highlighted the joy and comfort it must have brought to the Lord when the shadow of the cross loomed so near.

This lovely gesture was made when "the chief priests and the teachers of the law were looking for some sly way to arrest Jesus and kill him" (v. 1). The implacable hatred of religious man served as a black backdrop to the devoted love of a disciple.

The scene closes on an equally somber note: "Then Judas Iscariot, one of the Twelve, went to the chief priests to betray Jesus to them. They were delighted to hear this, and promised to give him money. So he watched for an opportunity to hand him over" (vv. 10-11).

Between those two sordid events, there was enacted one of the most moving scenes of the Lord's life.

The identity of the anonymous woman has been widely debated, but there are some grounds for thinking it may have been Mary of Bethany, and I will follow that idea.

In the gospels, women often had a special ministry to the Lord, and this was one of those occasions. In the East it was a common practice to sprinkle a few drops of oil on the head of a guest. The oil would cost only a few cents.

A feast was being held in the Lord's honor in the home of Simon the leper. Was he the father of Martha, Mary, and Lazarus? Did he, as a leper, live in a separate house? These are questions to which Scripture gives no answer.

While Jesus was reclining at the table, Mary "came with an alabaster jar of very expensive perfume, made of pure nard. . . . and poured the perfume on his head" (v. 3).

This was the most costly of all fragrant oils in the world. Some ingredients came from the distant Himalayas, and it was reserved for the use of royalty and the very rich. Mark records that its value was more than one year's wages.

Stop and think of the average wage, and you will have an idea of the cost to Mary of her impulsive act of love. In a moment of time she had spent more than a year's wages, seemingly for no useful purpose. The significant thing was that she did not pour only a few drops on her Lord's head. She broke the neck of the beautiful jar and, with lavish hand, poured all the perfume on His head.

THE DISCIPLES' ASSESSMENT

"Why this waste of perfume?" (v. 4).

It was sheer extravagance. Why should the woman be so lavish, when a few drops would have sufficed?

Prudence and parsimony, with cold calculation, would dictate how much (or how little) would be sufficient for the occasion. To them it was a matter of profit and loss. To Mary it was the supreme moment of her life, the moment when she avowed her pure love for her Lord.

Had Mary used only a few drops of perfume as they suggested, the story would never have been passed down through the centuries. Nor would other hearts be stimulated to a similar expression of the love that means so much to the Lord. Do we calculatingly reckon up our gifts to Him, carefully measuring out the expenditure of time and strength we devote to the interest of His kingdom? His heart aches for the abandon of love, and His work languishes when it is absent.

David set an example for us when he refused to accept the threshing-floor of Araunah as a gift. "Shall I give to the Lord that which costs me nothing?" he protested.

"Why this waste of perfume?"

It was waste. Why not do something useful with the money it would bring on the market? Why not be practical? "You serve God best by serving His creatures." Think of the number of poor people it would have fed! True, it would have fed many, but thank God it was not sold.

In His ministry Jesus had demonstrated abundantly that He was not indifferent to the plight of the poor. He was constantly ministering to their physical as well as their spiritual needs. It must have hurt Mary deeply when they so harshly rebuked her.

There had been several options open to her: (1) she could have sold the perfume—and turned it into hard cash and done something "useful" with it; (2) she could have saved it as provision for her old age; (3) she could have used it on herself, to enhance her beauty in the Lord's eyes; (4) she might have been like Nicodemus, and left it until too late.

Are there not somewhat similar options open to us in our relationship to the Lord?

"What a waste!" they said when the brilliant young Cambridge scholar Henry Martyn, who at the age of twenty had gained the highest award in mathematics the world had to offer, threw away his prospects for seven years of missionary work. But in those seven years he gave the world the New Testament in three of the major languages of the East.

"What a waste," they said when William Borden, heir to the Borden millions, turned his back on his alluring prospects to become a missionary to the Muslims and died before he reached the field. But that proved to be fruitful waste, for his biography, *Borden of Yale,* has influenced thousands toward the mission field.

Perhaps God is not so economical and utilitarian as we are. What waste and prodigality we see in His creation. But there are some things of the heart and the spirit that cannot be measured in cold cash.

How much do we know in practice of this seemingly wasteful and extravagant expenditure of ourselves in His service out of simple love for Him? Or are we niggardly and calculating in our self-giving? "He who sows sparingly shall reap sparingly."

HER OWN ASSESSMENT

The jar of perfume was her own prized possession. It may have been a family heirloom. She was under no necessity to expend it on the Lord. She might have used it to draw attention to herself, but she did not.

Are we using God's gifts to us for our own adornment, or are we pouring them out at His feet? Mary's was the spontaneous, uncalculating action of self-forgetful love. Her greatest delight was to bestow her choicest treasure on One she dearly loved.

One of the missionaries of the Overseas Missionary Fellowship lay dying of cancer. Her only daughter was about to sail for the mission field when the disease struck. Naturally, the daughter wanted to stay and nurse her mother in her hour of need. The mother could have kept her "jar of fragrance" for herself, yet its sweetness would have been spoiled for her. She would not let her daughter postpone her sailing. The people without Christ in that far-off land were in greater need than she was. To her, nothing was too precious for Jesus.

CHRIST'S ASSESSMENT

Jesus rebuked the disciples as sharply as they had rebuked Mary: "Leave her alone. . . . Why are you bothering her? She has done a beautiful thing to me. The poor you will always have with you, and you can help them any time you want. But you will not always have me" (vv. 6-7).

Of course we must care for the poor, but the Son of God, away from His home, longed for some personal expression of love; something done for Himself alone, out of pure, self-forgetful love. And Mary gave Him just that. Otherwise the pouring of the perfume would have been purposeless. It still means much to the Lord when He finds someone with a heart like Mary's.

"She did what she could," Jesus said of her action. There were many things that as a woman she could not do; but she did what she could. She poured her perfume on His head as an act of love while He was able to appreciate it.

Christ's prediction in verse 9 has been wonderfully fulfilled: "Wherever the gospel is preached *throughout the whole world,* what she has done will also be told, in memory of her." Implicit in this statement is the invincible confidence Jesus had that His disciples would carry His gospel "into the whole world." And we are the beneficiaries of that promise. The fragrance from that broken jar has reached us two thousand years later.

Her act won no applause from her companions, but to her beloved Master it was a refreshing oasis in the midst of the desert of man's indifference and hatred.

Have we ever offered a gift, done an act, emptied our jar of perfume out of pure love for Him alone? This He treasures more than all our service, for it is the love behind the service that makes the fragrance.

10

THE DISCIPLE'S MATURITY

"Let us . . . go on to maturity" (Hebrews 6:1).

God's revealed purpose is to produce disciples who will reflect the perfect humanity of His Son in both personal life and Christian service. This is an alluring prospect; yet the example of our Lord's life is so far above the level of our attainment that it is not difficult to become discouraged at the slowness of our progress.

The maturity He has in view is not confined to the spiritual life, for it must be lived out in the context of the body. This means more than the popular motto Let Go and Let God, for moral effort on our part is involved —moral effort, but not purely self-effort.

Bishop Westcott, in his commentary on Hebrews, brings out that point. He suggests that "Let us . . . go on to maturity" is capable of three translations, each of which is a warning against a peril:

We may stop too soon. We may feel we have arrived. But the writer rules out complacency as Paul did —"Not that I have already attained" (Philippians 3:12). No! "Let us go on." There are further heights to scale.

We may succumb to discouragement and drop our bundle as John Mark did. No! "Let us keep pressing on."

We may feel we have to achieve it alone. No! "Let us be borne on." In our pursuit of spiritual maturity, we have the cooperation of the Triune God. We are not left

to our paltry efforts but have the promised working of
the Holy Spirit to enable us to do His good pleasure.

It takes all three meanings to convey the rich meaning of the text. Maturity in the spiritual realm is not attained overnight, any more than it is in the physical. It is
a dynamic process that continues throughout life.

AIDS TO MATURITY

The aspiring disciple should, like a student, be prepared to work through his courses. There is no such thing
as instant maturity. It will involve the same diligence and
discipline as does a college course if we are to graduate
in the school of God.

There are certain things we must do for ourselves;
God will not do them for us. While the motto Let Go and
Let God emphasizes one aspect of truth, it can be a dan-
gerous half-truth and induce an unwholesome passivity.
Self-discipline and perseverance are essential ingredients.

Excellence in the realm of the intellect or music or
sport is not alone the work of the teacher; it involves the
active cooperation of the student and cannot be achieved
without strong motivation and deliberate self-denial.

No rapid growth in Christian maturity will be attained until the first indispensable step of *submission to
the lordship* of Christ has been taken. The key question
that determines whether or not He has been given that
place of authority in the life is, "Who makes the decisions?"

What dynamics will bear us on to maturity? "We,
who with unveiled faces all reflect [or behold] the Lord's
glory, are being transformed into His likeness with ever-
increasing glory, which comes from the Lord, who is the
Spirit" (2 Corinthians 3:18).

The *objective* means, "beholding the glory of the
Lord," produces a *subjective* result, transformation in
the disciple who practices it. We tend to become like

those we admire. Robert Murray McCheyne used to say, "A glance at Christ will save, but it is the gazing at Christ that sanctifies." This necessarily means that time will be set aside to enable the Spirit to effect the transformation.

While we spend time gazing at the Christ who is revealed in the Scriptures and long to be more like Him, the Holy Spirit silently effects the progressive change. He achieves that by increasing our aspiration, and revealing and imparting the graces and virtues of our Lord in response to our trust.

ACCEPTING EXTERNAL DISCIPLINES

Some experiences of life will greatly accelerate the maturing process. Although the three Hebrew youths (Daniel 3:16-29) must have been mystified by God's failure to intervene on their behalf, they matured rapidly in the fiery furnace experience. And so can we in our trials. Our attitude will determine whether God's disciplines are bane or blessing, whether they sweeten or sour.

Samuel Rutherford wrote, "O what I owe to the furnace, fire and hammer of my Lord!" God orders the circumstances of our lives with meticulous care. He never makes a mistake.

The presence or absence of spiritual maturity is never more noticeable than in one's attitude to the changing circumstances of life. Too often they generate anxiety, anger, frustration, or bitterness, whereas God's design is always for our spiritual growth. "God disciplines us for our good" (Hebrews 12:10). Someone said, "There is something about maturity that comes through adversity. If you don't suffer a little, you will never stop being a kid!"

Paul's testimony to that truth was hammered out on the anvil of tough experience. Read the catalog of his trials in 2 Corinthians 11:23-28, and then hear him say,

> *I have learned* to be content whatever the circum-
> stances. I know what it is to be in need, and I know
> what it is to have plenty. *I have learned the secret* of
> being content in any and every situation, whether well
> fed or hungry, whether living in plenty or in want. (Phi-
> lippians 4:11-12; italics added)

That is spiritual maturity. Needless to say, Paul did
not reach that victorious position overnight. It was a costly learning process, but through dependence on the Holy
Spirit, he mastered that very difficult lesson. The same
Spirit and the same grace are available to us.

At a gathering of aging Christians, the speaker startled them by saying, "It is not your arteries that are your
problem, it is your attitudes." There is more than a grain
of truth in his assertion. William Barclay tells of a woman who had recently lost her husband. A sympathetic
friend, in trying to be comforting, said, "Sorrow does col-
or life, doesn't it?"

"Yes, indeed it does," was the response, "but I in-
tend to choose the colors!" She was well along the road
to recovery from her grief. The colors she chose were
neither black nor purple.

In the days of the early church, there were four attitudes that people adopted toward the trials and sufferings of life.

The *fatalist* regarded whatever happened as inevitable and unalterable, so why fight against it? Why not ignore it? The Muslim fatalist dismisses it with: "It is the
will of Allah!"

The *Stoic's* outlook was that, since you can do nothing about it, harden yourself, defy the circumstances, and
let them do their worst.

The *Epicurian's* attitude was, "Let us eat, drink, and
be merry, for tomorrow we die." Let us ameliorate our
sufferings by indulging in the sensual pleasures of life.

The *mature disciple*, however, goes far beyond
grimly submitting to the inevitable and unalterable will

of God. He or she not only accepts the will of God but embraces it joyously, even though it be through tears.

Regarding Paul's mastery of his circumstances, note that it was a process, not a crisis. His mastery covered every type of circumstance from plenty to want. The secret of which he spoke is found in Philippians 4:13: "I can do everything through him who gives me strength." It was because of his vital union with Christ that he was able to triumph and be content. He did not run away from the difficult circumstance but embraced it and made it tributary to his spiritual growth. Because he was so dependent on Christ, he could be independent of circumstances.

DEVELOPING RIGHT ATTITUDES TOWARD TEMPTATION

God uses even the temptations that come from Satan to produce strong and mature character. As used in the King James Version, the word *temptation* is applied to the activity of both God and Satan. In the original languages, two parallel Hebrew and Greek words are used, but each in a different sense. Their meaning is: (1) *to test*, as seen in the refining process that separates the dross and alloy from the pure gold. This testing is sent from God and is always employed in a good sense; (2) *to tempt* or probe, in order to find a weak spot that is open to attack. It is almost always used in a bad sense. Since God never tempts man to evil (James 1:13), this is the activity of Satan.

In the experience of Joseph, both aspects synchronized, and the two conflicting experiences can be traced. Joseph himself, in reviewing his past, was able to say to his brothers, "You intended to harm me, but God intended it for good" (Genesis 50:20).

Satan tempts and seduces the disciple to sin. God tests the disciple to produce the gold of proved character and lead him to greater spiritual maturity. James tells us the correct attitude to testing: "Consider it pure joy, my brothers, whenever you face trials of many kinds, because you know that the testing of your faith develops perseverance. . . . Blessed is the man who perseveres under trial" (James 1:2, 12).

The classic text on temptation is:

> God is faithful; he will not let you be tempted beyond what you can bear. But when you are tempted, he will also provide a way out so that you can stand up under it. (1 Corinthians 10:13)

That passage is full of comfort for the tempted soul. It tells us four things about God that will provide a mainstay in temptation's hour.

He is faithful. He will not abandon those who trustfully look to Him for help and keeping. He will be unfailingly true to His Word.

He is sovereign. He controls the circumstances of life and will limit the strength of the temptation, for He knows our individual "load limit." That gives us assurance that we will be able to stand the strain.

He is impartial. He allocates tests that are "common to man." In the heat of temptation, many feel that they are the only ones to experience such a trial, but it is not so. Although the exact temptation may be different, the same principles and escape hatches are open to all alike.

He is powerful. He has an escape route from every kind of temptation. The key to the door is hanging nearby. Defeat is avoidable. The word translated "stand up under it," or "endure," means "to pass through unscathed." We must, however, be watchful for the enemy's snares and wiles, for he is subtle and underhanded in his methods.

Our enemy chooses his timing shrewdly. The temptation to discouragement and flight came to Elijah when he was totally exhausted both physically and emotionally. Joseph was tempted by Potiphar's wife when there were no men in the house and nobody else would have known. Jonah found the ship to Tarshish ready and waiting when he was disobediently running away from the divine command. David was tempted when he was neglecting his kingly duties and indulging in illegitimate relaxation. Jesus was tempted by Satan when He had fasted for forty days and was under intolerable spiritual pressure.

Satan chose the occasion in each case with diabolical skill, so that it would come with maximum impact. How important, then, is Peter's warning: "Be self-controlled and alert. Your enemy the devil prowls around like a roaring lion looking for someone to devour" (1 Peter 5:8).

CULTIVATING RIGHT HABITS

In one sense, life consists largely of making habits and breaking habits, for we are all creatures of habit. We are unconsciously forming and fracturing habits all the time, and for that reason this area of life must be brought under Christ's control. It is an essential part of the soul's education.

It is helpful to remember that after conversion we are no longer unregenerate personalities. As Paul wrote, "If anyone is in Christ, he is a new creation; the old has gone, the new has come!" (2 Corinthians 5:17). We are now indwelt by the Holy Spirit, whose supreme desire is to make us like Christ. To that end, God has promised to supply both the impulse and the power.

"It is God who works in you to will and to act according to his good purpose" (Philippians 2:13). Our task is to relate these truths and promises to our making and breaking of habits.

We all have bad habits, some of which may be patently wrong. Others may not be inherently wrong but are unhelpful. Take, for example, the habit of not being punctual. Some people are always late. They seem to have no concern about the amount of other people's time they waste. It has become an ingrained habit. Such people should seriously face the consequences to others of their delinquency, for it is that. They should form an inflexible purpose to push their program ten minutes earlier, break the old habit, and form a new one. The aid of the Holy Spirit is always available in the forming of a new and good habit, but it is we who must do it. God does not act instead of us: it is a partnership.

God gives the soil, the seed, the rain. Man supplies the skill, the toil, the sweat. In other words, the disciple must work out what God works in (Philippians 2:12).

In the culture of the soul, no habit is more crucial and formative than maintaining a consistent devotional life—a regular time reserved for fellowship and communion with God. Not everyone finds that easy, but its importance and value cannot be exaggerated. Since that is the case, it is only reasonable to expect that the habit will be the focus of relentless attack from our adversary.

Although it may not always be possible, there is both logical and spiritual value in observing the first hour of the day.

> Or e'er a word or action
> Has stained its snowy scroll,
> Bring the new day to Jesus
> And consecrate the whole.
> Then fear not for the record
> He surely will indite,
> Whatever Jesus doeth,
> It shall be, must be, right.

Later hours of the day have routine duties that must be performed. Interruptions often break the routine, but in spite of these, it is most helpful to establish a regular routine that enables one to breathe the incense of heaven before inhaling the smog and fog of earth.

In the quiet hour the mind can be adjusted before meeting people or facing difficult problems. The day's duties and responsibilities can be committed to God. We can memorize a Scripture verse to chew on during the day. We should be alert to look for some special thought or message in our reading.

We can relate the principles of Scripture to the details of daily life, remembering that the Bible contains *principles* to guide, *commands* to obey, *warnings* to heed, *examples* to emulate, and *promises* to claim.

With regard to prayer in the quiet time, we should first seek to realize the presence of God. He encouraged us with the words "Draw near to God and He will draw near to you" (James 4:8, NASB). Communion has two sides, so silence is sometimes appropriate in order to hear the voice of God.

Pray audibly if that helps in concentration. If privacy is difficult to find, retire into the inner part of your being. In the evening, review the day with confession and thanksgiving, and let your last thoughts be of God.

11
THE DISCIPLE'S OLYMPICS

"Take time and trouble to keep yourself spiritually fit" (1 Timothy 4:7, Phillips).

The Olympic Games are not usually associated with anything of a religious nature, but those staged in Melbourne, Australia, in 1956 were a notable exception. A striking feature of the spectacular opening ceremony was the deeply impressive singing by massed choirs of the "Hallelujah Chorus" from Handel's *Messiah.*

Although they were pagan in origin, there is much for the disciple to learn from the Pan-Hellenic games, of which the Olympics are the most famous. The New Testament writers, Paul in particular, drew many parallels between the training and performance of the competing athlete and the duties and privileges of the Christian. It is most probable that Paul would have had in mind the Isthmian Games, which were hosted by Corinth every third year. He was familiar with the rivalries and ambitions inherent in the sport, to which there are more than fifty references in the New Testament.

Every serious entrant to the Games then, as now, was determined to excel and to defeat his rivals. His aim was nothing short of winning the prize in his particular event.

Recently, I saw a young New Zealand cyclist win a grueling race in which he broke the national record. In a subsequent interview by the TV sports commentator, he was asked the question, "And what do you aim at for the future?" With not a moment's hesitation the reply came back: "I aim to be one of the best cyclists in the world."

In order to realize his ambition, he was prepared to pay any price in training—grueling discipline, forfeiture of social life, self-denial in many areas—and all for a piece of gold, or even bronze. Why is it that so few disciples have a similar, fixed ambition to excel for Christ? Are we "taking time and trouble to keep spiritually fit," or have we grown soft and flabby?

Immediately before his death, Polycarp, the saintly bishop of Smyrna, prayed: "O God, make me a true athlete of Jesus Christ, to suffer and to conquer." His prayer was answered in his martyrdom. In our sports-conscious world the great majority are only TV athletes, and too few are participators. Unfortunately, in large measure the same is true in the church.

The Indispensable Training

Take time and trouble to keep yourself spiritually fit. Bodily fitness has a limited value, but spiritual fitness is of unlimited value, for it holds promise both for this present life and for the life to come. (1 Timothy 4:8, Phillips)

In writing to his Corinthian friends, Paul reminded them that "every competitor in athletic events goes into serious training. Athletes will take tremendous pains—for a fading crown of leaves" (1 Corinthians 9:25, Phillips). It was an inflexible condition of entering the Olympic Games that the athlete undergo ten months of rigorous training. No exceptions were tolerated.

During those months, they had to live rigorously disciplined lives, bridling their normal desires and refraining from certain pastimes that might affect their fitness.

They had to have a balanced diet and get rid of all super-fluous fat. In our day the more popular outlook is: "Do your own thing. If it feels good, do it." This is not the way athletes for Christ are produced.

The actual rules of the contest were recorded by Horace. "There must be ordinary living, but spare food. Abstain from confections. Make a point of exercising at the appointed times in heat and cold. Drink neither cold water nor wine at random. Give yourself to the training master as to a physician, and then enter the contest."

What challenging words these are to the lax and un-disciplined disciple.

In reality there should be no such thing as an undis-ciplined disciple. Both words come from the same root, yet discipline has become the ugly duckling in modern society.

A great deal of prominence is given to the Holy Spir-it today, and rightly so. But little prominence is given to Galatians 5:22-23: "the fruit of the Spirit is . . . [disci-pline] self-control." One of the clearest evidences that the Holy Spirit is working in power in our lives is seen not merely in our emotional experience, but in an in-creasingly disciplined life-style.

The athlete who aspires to win the coveted prize does not indulge himself. He is prepared to take a stand against the spirit of this godless age. Is it not suspicious that while people will applaud and admire the sacrifice, discipline, and self-control of the athlete, they are turned off when it is suggested that there should be a compara-ble dedication on the part of the disciple of the disci-plined Christ?

The word Paul uses for "train" in 1 Timothy 4:7 is that from which we get our word *gymnasium*—the place where the athlete learns to harden his muscles, prolong his wind, and gain flexibility. The Holy Spirit urges each of us to do in the spiritual sphere what the athlete does in the gymnasium. It is commendable that so many are taking up aerobics today. It would be beneficial to the disciple to be equally zealous in spiritual aerobics.

A pampered body means a lost race. A flabby athlete gains no medals. Augustine knew this. He had a prayer that he often offered:

> O God, that I might have towards my God,
> a heart of flame;
> Towards my fellow-men a heart of love;
> Towards myself, a heart of steel.

OLYMPICS FOR THE AGING

It is encouraging for those of us who are older to realize that God is not exclusively youth-oriented. In thinking of the Olympic contests, we automatically associate them with virile youth. They are the athletes.

But in his reference to the Games, Paul viewed himself as nearing the end of the race—but still in training. Hear his words:

> Do you remember how, on the racing-track, every competitor runs, but only one wins the prize? Well, you ought to run with your minds fixed on winning the prize! . . . *I run the race then with determination. I am no shadow-boxer, I really fight!* I am my body's sternest master, for fear that when I have preached to others I should myself be disqualified. (1 Corinthians 9:24-27, Phillips; italics added)

Thank God we older disciples are not out of the race! We entered the race at conversion. At first it may have seemed to be a 100-meter dash, but we have proved it to be a 26-mile marathon that has tested our perseverance and spiritual stamina. And now it is for us still to "run with perseverance the race marked out for us" (Hebrews 12:1) so that we might win the prize.

It is easy to grow lax and less disciplined as the years go by. Are we mentally lazy and undisciplined? Do we feel we have earned the right to drop out of the race? Not that way went the Crucified, and not that way went the men and women who have counted for God.

> God, harden me against myself,
> The coward with pathetic voice.

OLYMPIC RULES

> If anyone competes as an athlete, he does not receive the victor's crown unless he competes according to the rules. (2 Timothy 2:5)

Mastery of the rules of the contest is a first priority for the athlete. Unless he conforms to them there will be no prize. Enforcing this condition, Augustine challenged a runner: "You may be making great strides, but are you running outside the track?"

How diligently the aspiring driver studies the provisions of the *Rules of the Road!* Are we equally diligent in mastering and conforming to the rules governing the Christian race?

The Christian athlete's rule book is, of course, the New Testament. In it he will find all the guidance he needs for what is allowable and what is not. But this Book has an advantage over the Olympic book of rules; it promises adequate power to enable the runner to complete the race. Paul availed himself of that power, and on reaching the tape he was able to testify: "I have fought the good fight, I have finished the race" (2 Timothy 4:7).

OBSTACLES IN THE RACE

"You were running well," wrote Paul to the Galatians. "Who hindered you from obeying the truth?" (5:7, NASB).

There are many influences to deflect us from reaching the goal. We have a wily adversary who will draw on his six millennia of nefarious experience to lure us from the track.

There is an interesting Greek story of Atlanta and Hippomenes. The fleet-footed Atlanta challenged any young man to a race. The reward of victory would be her hand in marriage. The penalty of defeat would be death. She must have been a very attractive girl, for a number of men accepted the challenge, only to lose the race and their lives as well.

Hippomenes, too, accepted her challenge, but before setting out on the race, he secreted on his person three golden apples. When the race began, Atlanta easily outstripped him. He took out a golden apple and rolled it in front of her. The glitter of the gold caught her eye, and as she stopped to pick it up, he shot past her. She quickly recovered and again outdistanced him. Another golden apple rolled across her track, and again she stopped to pick it up, allowing Hippomenes again to sweep past her. The goal was near and he was ahead, but once more she overtook him. Seizing his last chance, he rolled the third apple, and while Atlanta wavered, Hippomenes reached the tape. They were married and lived happily ever after!

Our wily adversary is adept in deploying his golden apples. He does not observe the rules of the game, and he will use every subtlety to prevent our winning the prize. But Paul had every reason to claim, "We are not unaware of his schemes" (2 Corinthians 2:11). Not all of us are able to make a similar assertion. Too many are spiritual illiterates when it comes to discerning and anticipating his subtleties.

The writer of the letter to the Hebrews was aware of the obstacles and hindrances the athlete would meet and urged his readers: "Therefore, since we are surrounded by such a great cloud of witnesses, let us throw off everything that hinders and the sin that so easily entangles, and let us run with perseverance the race marked out for us" (Hebrews 12:1).

It was customary for the Olympic athlete to discard his flowing robes—his track suit—before he went to the track. Those garments were cumbersome and would impede progress, so he threw them off and ran almost naked.

In our own race, have we thrown off every entangling and hindering thing—the besetting and upsetting sins that prevent progress toward spiritual maturity? That is not something God does, but something we must do with full purpose of will. Satan's lures come to us along the main avenues of appetite, avarice, and ambition. We should check to see whether any of Satan's golden apples operate in any of those areas of our lives.

FIXITY OF AIM

"Let us fix our eyes on Jesus, the author and perfector of our faith" (Hebrews 12:2).

The Greek foot race was regarded as the sharpest and most violent physical exercise then known. In one race, Addas, the victor, burst over the finishing line a motionless heap of muscle—dead. The exertion had overextended his physical reserves. Winning a race makes great demands on the stamina and perseverance of the athlete.

Once the race has begun, the athlete cannot afford to look back. He must press on to the tape without distraction. His eyes must be fixed on the umpire's stand at the end of the track if he is to win the prize. That was the background of Paul's notable statement "One thing I do: Forgetting what is behind and straining toward what is ahead, I press on toward the goal to win the prize for which God has called me heavenward in Christ Jesus" (Philippians 3:13-14).

So must the disciple run his race with eyes steadfastly fixed on his encouraging Lord, who is at once Judge, Umpire, and Awarder. He is not to look back either wistfully or hopelessly but to resolutely forget what is behind—failures and disappointments as well as successes and victories. He must strain forward to the tape with eyes fixed on his welcoming Lord. It was He who initiated our faith, and it is He who will strengthen us to complete the course.

After employing the figure of the runner in 1 Corinthians 9:25, Paul turns to the sport of boxing: "I do not run like a man running aimlessly; I do not fight like a man beating the air. No, I beat my body and make it my slave" (1 Corinthians 9:26-27).

Boxing was one of the sports in the Pentathlon at the Olympic Games, and Paul used it to illustrate his own attitude toward his body, which was so often the focus of temptation. He realized that his greatest foe lodged in his own breast: "I know that nothing good lives in me, that is, in my sinful nature" (Romans 7:18).

> There is a man who often stands
>   'twixt me and Thy glory.
> His name is Self, my carnal Self
>   stands 'twixt me and Thy glory.
> O mortify him! mortify him!
>   Put him down, my Saviour;
>   Exalt Thyself alone,
> Lift high the standard of the cross
>   and 'neath its folds
> Conceal the standard-bearer.
>   (Anonymous)

In some Eastern cities, as one walks along the street in the darkness of early morning, it is a common sight to see men with clenched fists, punching the empty air. But there is nothing to fear from them. They are only shadowboxers.

Paul disclaimed being a shadowboxer. "I land every blow," he claimed, "and the blows land on my own body. Thus I make it my slave and not my master."

THE PRIZE

"Run in such a way as to get the prize" (1 Corinthians 9:24).

What moves the athlete to exercise such self-discipline and exhibit such feats of strength and endurance? Surely it will be a large purse or some trophy of great value. But no. "They do it to obtain a crown that will not last"—a mere chaplet of laurel leaves, of no intrinsic value at all. And yet it was the most coveted of all the honors the nation could confer. Cicero maintained that the Olympic victor received more honor than the returning conquering general. But it was a prize that did not last.

The gorgeous Olympic pageant reached its climax when the crown of victory was placed on the victor's head by the umpire of the Games. Flowers and gifts were showered on him by his admirers.

With that scene in his mind, Paul anticipated the day when he would be crowned by the Judge of all the earth: "Now there is in store for me the crown of righteousness, which the Lord, the righteous Judge, will award to me on that day—and not only to me, but also to all who have longed for his appearing" (2 Timothy 4:8).

Throughout the years that he had run the race, Paul kept his gaze fixed on Christ. To receive from His nail-pierced hands the crown would be abundant compensation for all his sufferings. To hear his Lord and Master say, "Well done!" would make the self-renunciations seem as nothing.

Paul finished his brief paragraph about the Games on a serious note. Despite the vast scope of his achievements, he still recognized the subtlety of his enemy and the frailty of his own human nature. "I beat my body and make it my slave," he said, "so that after I have preached to others, I myself will not be disqualified for the prize" (1 Corinthians 9:27).

As he grew older, he found that the world was no less delusive, sin no less seductive, and the devil no less malicious than in his youth, and that caused him a wholesome fear.

The word *disqualified* had no reference to his salvation. He had no fear of losing that, but he did fear being disapproved or disqualified by the Judge, thus having run in vain. Let us entertain a similar, wholesome fear and "run so as to win the prize."

> Teach me Thy way, O Lord,
>   Teach me Thy way,
> Thy gracious aid impart,
>   Teach me Thy way
>
> Until my journey's done,
>   Until the race is run,
> Until the crown is won,
>   Teach me Thy way.
>   (B. M. R.)

12

THE DISCIPLE'S COMPASSION

"When he saw the crowds, he had compassion on them" (Matthew 9:36).

"Sit down, young man! When God purposes to save the heathen, He will do it without your help!"

God could doubtless have done it without the help of the young cobbler, but He didn't. He took an obscure young disciple from an obscure town, called and equipped him, and used him to initiate the modern missionary era.

William Carey was innocent of systematic theology and missiology at that stage, but he had qualities that uniquely equipped him for that strategic task. He had a passionate love for Christ and a compassionate love for those in distant lands who did not know Him.

As he worked away at his cobbler's bench, with a globe of the world in front of him, God was laying on his heart a great burden for the lost. The compassion that moved the Lord when He saw the crowds "harassed and helpless, like sheep without a shepherd," was reborn in William Carey's heart.

Not all Christians, even in evangelical circles, believe that all men and women without Christ are lost. A creeping universalism is gaining ground. Many feel that, at the last, God's love will triumph over His wrath, and He will save all men. One does not impugn the motives of those who embrace this view, but the crucial question is, Is that what Christ and the apostles clearly taught in the Scriptures?

Scripture nowhere states or implies that pagan people will be lost simply because they have not heard the gospel. Multiplied millions have never had the opportunity. If pagan people are lost, it is for exactly the same reason as you and I were lost—because they, like us, are sinful by nature and by practice. Paul makes this crystal clear: *"There is no difference,* for all have sinned and fall short of the glory of God"* (Romans 3:22-23; italics added).

THOSE WHO HAVE NEVER HEARD

Paul draws no distinction between those who have heard the gospel and those who have not. All are equally lost because all are equally sinful. "God has concluded all under sin," and this fact enables Him to offer mercy to all who will receive it.

This is not the place to enlarge upon this subject, the implications of which are so painful and on which there are conflicting views, but those who hold universalistic views have some questions to answer.

1. Was the Lord's statement "I am the way. . . . No one comes to the Father except through me" (John 14:6), relative or absolute? Can men come to a Father of whom they have never heard?
2. When Jesus said, "No one can enter the kingdom of God unless he is born of water and the Spirit" (John 3:5), did He have unrevealed exceptions in mind? Are pagans automatically born again without their consent?
3. What did Paul mean when he reminded the Ephesian Christians of their condition as heathen and said, "Remember that . . . you were separate from Christ

... without hope and without God in the world"?
(Ephesians 2:12; italics added).

4. Is there scriptural warrant for saying that the names
   of the heathen are automatically inscribed in the Book
   of Life (Revelation 20:12)? If so, would not that rather
   argue for not giving them the gospel, lest they reject it
   as so many do?
5. Was John deluded when he wrote that the portion of
   those who practiced magic arts (witchcraft) and all
   idolaters will be in the fiery lake of burning sulphur
   (Revelation 21:8)?
6. What did Paul mean when he posed the four devastating questions of Romans 10:13-15?
   "Everyone who calls on the name of the Lord will be
   saved," he announced.
   "How, then, can they call on the one they have not
   believed in?
   "And how can they believe in the one of whom they
   have not heard?
   "And how shall they hear without someone preaching
   to them?
   "And how can they preach unless they are sent?"
   Was he just indulging in heartless casuistry, or is
   there an answer?

These scriptures and others, on the face of them,
seem to present a *prima facie* case for the lost state of
unevangelized pagans. If the salvation of lost men and
women is so serious that it demanded the sufferings of
Christ on the cross, then how serious is their condition
and how urgent should be our endeavor to relieve it?

Other scriptures, of course, make clear that the responsibility of those who have not heard the gospel is immeasurably less than that of those who have heard and
rejected it. In the light of Calvary, we can rest in the assurance that "the Judge of all the earth [will] do right"
(Genesis 18:25).

Heathen Ignorance Not Total

In point of fact, the heathen are not so ignorant and their sin not so involuntary as some may think. A friend of mine who was a missionary in Zaire, when it was known as the Belgian Congo, wished to discover the degree of light enjoyed by a raw pagan who had had no contact with Europeans or Christians. He went with an interpreter to a village that had never been visited by a white man. After establishing rapport he asked, in terms the chief could understand, what things he considered to be sin. Without hesitation, the chief replied, "Murder, theft, adultery, witchcraft."

That meant that every time he indulged in any of those practices, he knew he was sinning against the light he had. Was this not what Paul said?

> Indeed, when Gentiles, who do not have the law, do by nature things required by the law, they are a law for themselves, even though they do not have the law, since *they show that the requirements of the law are written on their hearts,* their consciences also bearing witness, and their thoughts now accusing, now even defending them. (Romans 2:14-16; italics added)

Since that is the case, every disciple of the compassionate Christ will be concerned to see that the unevangelized millions will have an opportunity to hear the gospel.

It was when Jesus saw the crowds of people who thronged Him, "without hope and without God," that He had compassion on them.

The Three Essentials

John Ruskin, famous poet and art critic, once said that a good artist must possess three qualities: (1) *an eye to see* and appreciate the beauty of the scene he desires to catch on canvas; (2) *a heart to feel* and register the beauty and atmosphere of the scene; (3) *a hand to perform*—to transfer to canvas what the eye has seen and the heart felt.

Are not they three of the qualities most essential to the disciple in his work for the Master?

An eye to see the spiritual need of the men and women around us. Physical need is much more readily discerned than is spiritual need because it makes a visual impression on us, whereas spiritual need is sensed only by those who are spiritual.

How did Jesus see His world? "When he saw the crowds, he had compassion on them." He saw a crowded world. It has been estimated that in our Lord's time, the population of the world was about 250 million. What kind of world do we see? Five thousand million—twenty times as many!

He saw a *helpless* world. How contemporary! With all our sophistication, we move helplessly from one crisis to another, with few solutions. Those people were bewildered, crushed by injustice and oppression. His heart ached for them in their inability to improve their spiritual condition.

He saw a *shepherdless* world. Sheep have no sense of direction, no weapon of offense or defense. Jesus saw them as lost, with no one to care for their spiritual destitution. And are there not still vast numbers in the less developed countries who are in the same condition?

When worldly men see a crowd, each sees something different. The educator sees potential students. The politician, potential voters. The merchant, potential customers. Each sees them with the thought of the way they can profit from them. Jesus never exploited any man for His own benefit. "When He saw them he had compassion on them." And soon that compassion would lead Him to the cross.

Eyes that look are common. Eyes that see are rare. Do we have eyes that see?

We need *a heart to feel* for the spiritual needs of men and women. Compassion is much more than pity. That kind of emotion by no means always leads to loving action. The word *compassion* means "to suffer together with." It is the Latin form of the Greek word that gives us *sympathy,* and it implies identification with its object.

A. W. Tozer once said that there was abroad an irresponsible pursuit of happiness and that most people would rather be happy than feel the wounds of other people's sorrows. That is borne out by the almost pathological pursuit of happiness by the crowds. But they miss the true Source of joy and satisfaction.

If we keep sensitively in touch with the Christ of the broken heart we will share His concern. Compassion is the language of the heart and is intelligible in any tongue. It is not difficult, however, to be so engrossed in our own lives that our hearts become calloused and insensitive to the needs of others.

Television has had a deleterious effect on the emotions of many of its devotees. Constant familiarity with scenes of tragedy, horror, violence, and simulated emotion has made their emotions so superficial that it is difficult for them to feel anything deeply. We see terrible scenes, are shocked for a few moments, and then turn to the next program. We have grown emotionally superficial, and that has spilled over into the spiritual life.

Luke tells us that when Jesus "approached Jerusalem and saw the city, He wept over it" (Luke 19:41). His compassion was not dry-eyed. How different from the Greek gods! They came to earth to enjoy and indulge themselves. The Son of God expressed His concern in salty tears. As He foresaw the future doom of the city when judgment would fall on it for its sin and impenitence, His heart overflowed its banks.

What a concept—a weeping God! Tears streamed down His face in compassion for the very men who shortly would crucify Him outside that city! Imagine the incredulity of the angels. They were not the synthetic tears of television but tears of genuine concern for lost men and women.

Paul's ministry was not dry-eyed. He shared the passion and compassion of his Lord. When he bade the Ephesian Christians farewell, he said to them, "Remember that for three years I never stopped warning each of you night and day *with tears"* (Acts 20:31; italics added).

Do we share our Lord's concern and compassion?

A hand to perform, to act out our compassion. Christ's compassion was not stillborn; He did something about it. Seeing and feeling are sterile unless we are moved to action.

In the parable of the Good Samaritan, Jesus taught His disciples a memorable lesson in compassion (Luke 10:29-32). The robbers saw in the wounded traveler a victim to exploit; the priest and Levite, a nuisance to ignore; the lawyer who sparked the story saw a problem to be solved; the innkeeper, a customer from whom he could profit. The hated Samaritan saw him as a neighbor he could help in his hour of need.

> "Which of these three do you think was a neighbor to the man who fell into the hands of robbers?" The expert in the law replied, "The one who had mercy on him." Jesus told him, "Go and do likewise." (Luke 10:36-37)

The highest expression of compassion is compassionate action; otherwise, it is only stillborn sentiment.

The caring disciple whose eyes have been opened to see the plight of this lost world, whose heart has been moved by men's tragic condition, must swing into action.

George R. Murray, general director of the Bible Christian Union Mission, tells that up to the time he fully dedicated his life to the Lord he had been sincerely including God in his plans, but God wanted him to be included in *His* plan.

At a missionary prayer meeting at Columbia Bible College, it became clear that God's plan for him was full-time missionary service, preaching Christ where He was not known. It was then that he saw the world as God must see it. Before that time, he was willing to go but planning to stay. However, from that time on, his attitude was that he was planning to go but willing to stay. He soon had his call from God.

13

THE DISCIPLE'S PRAYER LIFE

"The Spirit helps us in our weakness. We do not know what we ought to pray for" (Romans 8:26).

Our Lord set the disciples such a glowing example in prayer that they pled with Him, "Lord, teach us to pray, just as John taught his disciples" (Luke 11:1). As they had heard Him pray, a yearning had sprung up in their hearts to know a similar intimacy with the Father. We do well to echo their request.

Prayer is an amazing paradox. It is a blending of simplicity and profundity. It can be an agony or an ecstasy. It can focus on a single objective, or it can roam the world. It is "the simplest form of speech that infant lips can try," and yet at the same time is "the sublimest strains that reach the Majesty on high." Small wonder, then, that even Paul, spiritual giant though he was, had to confess: "We do not know what we ought to pray for."

GOD'S INTERESTS MUST COME FIRST

To the maturing disciple, God's interests will always be paramount. The prayers of the immature Christian usually revolve around self. In response to the disciples' plea to be taught to pray, Jesus said, "This, then is how you should pray," and He gave them a pattern by which to model their prayers. It is noteworthy that in the prayer recorded in Matthew 6:9-13, the first half of the prayer is totally occupied with God and His interests. Only after that do personal petitions find a place. Worship, praise, and thanksgiving have first place. As would be expected, the prayers of Paul follow the Master's model.

THE DISCIPLE CAN PRAY WITH AUTHORITY

We are engaged in a relentless spiritual warfare that knows no truce. Our foes are unseen and intangible, but they are powerful. Against them only spiritual weapons will prevail. Paul wrote:

> We do not wage war as the world does. The weapons we fight with are not the weapons of the world. On the contrary, they have divine power to demolish strongholds. (2 Corinthians 10:3-4)

Of these weapons, prayer is the most formidable and potent in our conflict with "the spiritual forces of evil in the heavenly realms" (Ephesians 6:12).

> Restraining prayer, we cease to fight,
> Prayer makes the Christian's armour bright;
> And Satan trembles when he sees
> The weakest saint upon his knees.
>   (William Cowper)

The fulcrum on which defeat or victory turns is our ability to pray aright and make intelligent use of our weapons.

Jesus nowhere envisages His church in retreat. To the seventy eager disciples who returned from an evangelistic foray elated with their success, He made this powerful statement: "I saw Satan fall like lightning from heaven. *I have given you authority* to trample on snakes and scorpions, and *to overcome all the power of the enemy*" (Luke 10:18-19; italics added).

The unmistakable inference is that through the exercise of this delegated authority in their own sphere of service, the disciples, too, would see the overthrow of Satan. This promised authority was never withdrawn. But later, when the disciples lost faith in the promise, they were powerless to deliver a demon-possessed boy. They were paralyzed by their own unbelief. Jesus told them the remedy: "This kind can come out only by prayer" (Mark 9:29).

Restful and trustful prayer has an important place in the Christian life, but Paul taught and practiced a different kind of praying. Only strenuous and aggressive prayer that laid hold of the power released by the cross and the resurrection would dislodge the enemy from his age-long stronghold. It is that kind of praying that releases the power and resources of God and brings them into play in the field of battle.

Samuel Chadwick contended that Satan fears nothing from prayerless studies, teaching, and preaching. "He laughs at our toil, mocks at our wisdom, but trembles when we pray."

To the captious Pharisees, Jesus gave the illustration of a strong, well-armed man, feeling safe in his fortress: "How can anyone enter a strong man's house and carry off his possessions unless he first ties up the strong man? Then he can rob his house" (Matthew 12:29).

It is the responsibility of the disciple to exercise this delegated authority in prayer in his conflict with Satan and the power of darkness. In this way Christ's triumph becomes the triumph of His weakest follower.

THE DISCIPLE SHOULD PRAY AUDACIOUSLY

The mature disciple should be no stranger to this kind of praying. In the light of the wide-ranging promises to the intercessor, it is surprising that our prayers are so tepid. They seldom soar above past experience or natural thought. How seldom we pray for the unprecedented, let alone the impossible!

> Thou art coming to a King!
> Large petitions with thee bring,
> For His grace and power are such,
> None can ever ask too much.

Scripture bears witness to the fact that God delights to answer daring prayers that are based on His promises. Jesus encouraged His disciples to ask as freely for the impossible as the possible. He said to them, "If you have faith as small as a mustard seed, you can say to this mountain, 'Move from here to there' and it will move. Nothing will be impossible for you" (Matthew 17:20-21). All difficulties are the same size to God.

THE DISCIPLE WILL SOMETIMES WRESTLE IN PRAYER

"Epaphras, who is one of you and a servant of Christ Jesus. . . . is always wrestling in prayer for you" (Colossians 4:12).

That type of prayer is the experience of the mature disciple. Epaphras was one of these. But how pale a reflection of the praying of Epaphras are our prayers.

It is from the Greek word for "wrestle" that we derive our word *agonize*. It is used in the New Testament of men toiling until they are weary; of the athlete on the track, straining every muscle and nerve; of the soldier battling for his very life. This kind of prayer has been termed "an athletic of the soul."

THE DISCIPLE SHOULD PRAY WITH IMPORTUNITY

Jesus enforced the necessity of importunity and persistence in prayer by telling two parables—the three friends and the unprincipled judge. In each He taught by contrast, for God is neither a lazy, selfish neighbor, nor is He an unprincipled judge.

The three friends. In the parable recorded in Luke 11:5-8, one friend found himself in the embarrassing position of having no bread to set before a visitor who had dropped in on him unexpectedly. He hurried to a friend and asked for the loan of three loaves. From behind closed doors the "friend" replied that he was in bed and couldn't be bothered getting up to oblige him. However, the embarrassed host persisted until at last his lazy friend, because of his importunity, rose and gave him what he needed.

In applying the parable, Jesus contrasted by implication the surly selfishness of the reluctant friend with the willing generosity of His Father. If even an utterly selfish man, the argument ran, to whom sleep was more important than a friend's need, will reluctantly get up at midnight to comply with his friend's request because of his unabashed persistence, how much more will God be moved by the importunate entreaty of His children? (11:13).

The unprincipled judge. In the second parable, recorded in Luke 18:1-8, a widow who had been swindled took her case to court. The presiding judge was a man who "neither feared God nor cared about men." Time after time he rebuffed heartlessly the woman's entreaties for justice to be done. At last, exasperated by her persistence and in order to rid himself of the nuisance, he dealt with her case, and justice was done.

The argument is that if a nagging widow by her shameless persistence can overcome the obstinacy of an unprincipled judge, how much more will God's children receive the answer to their urgent prayers, since they are appealing, not to an adversary, but to a caring Advocate whose attitude is the antithesis of that of the uncaring judge.

Thus, by luminous parables Jesus depicted by way of contrast a true delineation of the character and attitude of His Father. He is not like an unjust judge who dispenses reluctant justice to a defrauded widow only because her persistence creates a nuisance.

The lesson to be drawn is that it is "shameless persistence" that comes away with full hands; and the opposite is also true. Tepid praying does not move God's arm. In contrast, John Knox cried, "Give me Scotland or I die." If our desire is so feeble that we can do without what we are asking and it is not something we must have at all costs, why should our prayer be answered?

Adoniram Judson of Burma said, "God loves an importunate prayer so much that He will not give us much blessing without it. He knows that it is a necessary preparation for our receiving the richest blessing He is longing to bestow.

"I never prayed sincerely and earnestly for anything but it came at some time, no matter how distant a day —somehow, in some shape, probably the last I would have devised, it came."

That naturally raises the question: Why can God not simply answer the prayer without requiring us to importune Him for an answer?

Why is importunity necessary?

God has assured us that there is no reluctance on His part to bestow any good gift. It is not that He wants to be coaxed. The repeated "how much more" in the above parables assures us of that. So the answer must be looked for elsewhere.

The necessity of importunity lies in us, not in God. William E. Biederwolf suggests that importunity is one of the instructors in God's training school for Christian culture. Sometimes He delays the answer because the petitioner is not in a fit state to receive it. There is something God desires to do in him first.

The Problem of Unanswered Prayer

The mature disciple will not stumble because of apparently unanswered prayer. He will not, however, adopt a fatalistic attitude; he will examine his prayers and seek to discover the cause of failure.

The plain fact is that God does not always say yes to every prayer (though we usually expect Him to do so). Moses entreated the Lord earnestly that he might enter the Promised Land. But God answered no (Deuteronomy 34:4). Paul prayed repeatedly that his "thorn in the flesh" might be removed, but God said no (2 Corinthians 12:7-9). However, He promised compensating grace. God is sovereign and all-wise, and we should be sensible enough and humble enough to recognize His sovereignty in the realm of prayer.

Our Lord's brother gives one reason for unanswered prayer: "When you ask, you do not receive, *because you ask with wrong motives*" (James 4:3; italics added). God does not undertake to answer every self-centered petition, but He does promise to answer every prayer that is according to His good and perfect will.

It may be that our prayer was not the prayer of faith, but only the prayer of hope. Jesus said, "According to your faith will it be done to you" (Matthew 9:29), not according to your hope. Are many of your prayers only prayers of hope?

Or we may have been substituting faith in prayer for faith in God. We are not told anywhere to have faith in prayer but to "have faith in God," the One who answers the prayer. This is more than a matter of semantics. Sometimes we sigh, "Our prayers are so weak and ineffective!" or, "My faith is so small!" Jesus anticipated this reaction when He said, "I tell you the truth, if you have faith as small as a mustard seed, you can say to this mountain, 'Move from here to there' and it will move. Nothing will be impossible for you" (Matthew 17:20).

The naked eye sees little difference between a grain of sand and a mustard seed, but there is a world of difference between the two. In one is the germ of life. It is not the size of our faith that is important, but is it a living faith in a living God?

The mature disciple will not become discouraged because of a delay in the answer to his prayer. He knows that a delayed answer is not necessarily a denied answer.

> Unanswered yet? Nay, do not say, ungranted,
>   Perhaps your part is not yet fully done.
> The work began when first your prayer was offered,
>   And God will finish what He has begun.
> If you will keep the incense burning there,
>   You shall have your desire—
>   Sometime, somewhere!
>   (Ophelia R. Browning)

God's timing is infallible. He takes every factor and contingency into account. We often want to pluck unripe fruit, but He will not be pressured into premature action.

If He in His wisdom delays the answer to our prayer, that delay will in the long run prove to be for our good (Hebrews 12:10). It will be either because He has some better thing for us, or because there is something He desires to achieve in our lives that can be effected in no other way.

As we mature spiritually and get to know our heavenly Father more intimately, we will be able to implicitly trust His love and wisdom, even when we cannot understand His actions. Jesus prepared His disciples for this experience when He said, "You do not realize now what I am doing, but later you will understand" (John 13:7).

14
THE DISCIPLE'S RIGHTS

"Don't we have the right . . . ? I have not used any of these rights" (1 Corinthians 9:3, 15).

Few would question the assertion that we should renounce the wrong things in our lives. It is self-evident that such things mar our lives, spoil our enjoyment of life, and limit our usefulness to God and man. But not everyone is equally convinced that in the interest of the gospel the disciple of Christ may need to renounce some things that are perfectly right and legitimate.

I once heard an arresting message on this theme preached by Rowland V. Bingham, founder of the Sudan Interior Mission, whose sacrificial missionary career gave him the right to speak with authority. Although it was sixty years ago, much that he said is still clear in my memory and colors this study.

Four times in 1 Corinthians 9 Paul asserts his rights in the gospel. Three times he claims that he has refrained from exercising these rights in the higher interests of spreading the gospel. He affirms that he is ready to forgo any right he may have, and forsake any privilege, out of love for Christ and in the interests of the progress of the gospel. Listen to the lengths to which he is prepared to go: *"We did not use this right.* On the contrary, we put up with anything rather than hinder the gospel of Christ"* (v. 12; italics added).

Oswald Chambers had some trenchant words to say in this connection: "If we are willing to give up only wrong things for Jesus, never let us talk about being in love with Him. Anyone will give up wrong things if he knows how, but are we prepared to give up the best we have for Jesus Christ? The only right a Christian has is the right to give up his rights. If we are to be the best for God, there must be victory in the realm of *legitimate desire* as well as in the realm of *unlawful indulgence.*"

Elsewhere the apostle insisted that everything that is legitimate is not necessarily helpful under all circumstances:

> Everything is permissible for me—but not everything is *beneficial.* (1 Corinthians 6:12; italics added)

> Everything is permissible, but not everything is *constructive.* (1 Corinthians 10:23; italics added)

He knew from experience that it was possible to indulge in permissible things to an inordinate degree and thus become a slave to them. So he adds yet another restraint:

> Everything is permissible for me, but I will not be *mastered* by anything. (1 Corinthians 6:12; italics added)

That means that the disciple must choose his priorities very carefully, even in things that are right in themselves. If we are aiming at the heights of Christian experience, there will always come the challenge to voluntary renunciation of some rights.

The Christian life is not the only realm in which this is the case. What renunciations the aspiring athlete is prepared to make in order to break a record or win a prize!

As in all else, our Lord set a shining example in His earthly life. As Son of God He was "heir of all things" and enjoyed rights and privileges beyond our dreaming. Yet for our sake He renounced them. Consider the stupendous surrender of rights involved in the Incarnation, when He "forsook the courts of everlasting day, and chose with us a darksome house of mortal clay."

A seventeenth-century poet depicts the scene when the Son of God renounced His rights to the enjoyment of the glories of His position as "heir of all things" in these vivid words:

> Hast thou not heard what my Lord Jesus did?
> Then let me tell you a strange storie.
> The God of power, when He did ride
> In His majestick robes of glorie,
> Resolved to light; and so one day
> He did descend, unrobing all the way.
> The starres His tires of light and rings obtained,
> The cloud His bow, the fire His spear,
> The sky His azure mantle gained.
> And when they asked what He would wear,
> He smiled, and said as He did go,
> He had new clothes amaking down below.
> (George Herbert)

On earth He surrendered His right to the comforts of home life, the right to the congenial company of heaven, and at the last, the right to life itself. The only rights He did not surrender were those essential to His role as Mediator between God and man. "I lay down my life for the sheep," Jesus claimed. "No one takes it from me, but I lay it down of my own accord" (John 10:15, 18). If sacrifice is "the ecstasy of giving the best we have to the one we love the most," it follows that at times there will be lower rights that must be renounced in favor of those that are higher.

Once a traveler has paid his fare, he is entitled to a seat on the bus. No one can legitimately take it from him. And when a mother with a baby in one arm and a bag of groceries in the other boards the crowded bus, he still has the right to keep his seat. But he also has the higher choice of giving it up to the lady. In the same way, at times the interests of the gospel—and that is Paul's pre-occupation in this passage—requires the renunciation of some of our rights.

Paul practiced what he preached. "Though I am free and belong to no man, I make myself a slave to everyone, to win as many as possible" (1 Corinthians 6:19). He makes reference to his personal rights in four areas, but he asserts that although he might have done so legiti-mately, he exploited none of them to the full (vv. 12, 15, 18).

THE RIGHT TO GRATIFY NORMAL APPETITE

"Don't we have the right to eat and drink?" he asked. He may have been asserting his liberty to eat cer-tain foods, for food offered to idols was a theme of the previous chapter. But the context would rather suggest that he is claiming the right to eat and drink at the ex-pense of the church—the right of the Christian worker to be maintained on the material level by those whom he serves in spiritual things.

But his question could be expanded to include not only food and drink but also all his normal physical appe-tites. Because they are bestowed by God, they are not unholy. In themselves they are legitimate, but they can be indulged in to such a degree or in such a relationship as to render them sinful. Because they are legitimate, that does not mean that we should always use our right to the full, much less abuse it.

The joy of sharing the gospel was to Paul of far greater importance than food or drink. When the inter-ests of the gospel demanded it, he gladly went hungry and thirsty. Hear his testimony: "I know what it is to be in need, and I know what it is to have plenty. I have learned the secret of being content in any and every situation, whether well-fed or hungry, whether living in plenty or in want" (Philippians 4:12).

Do we share his outlook? Have we discovered for ourselves his secret?

It can rightly be argued that a missionary has just as valid a right to rich and attractive food as any of his fellow-believers in the homeland. But there may be times when he may need to live at subsistence level if needy people are to be reached with the good news. His first priority must be the glory of God in the winning and discipling of souls.

John Wesley emulated the apostle Paul in his determination not to be enslaved by appetite. In order to gain this mastery, he lived solely on potatoes for two whole years. Apparently that did not affect his health adversely, for he lived to be eighty-nine years of age. He was no ascetic, but he would not tolerate being bossed by his appetite, especially if it would hinder the gospel of Christ (v. 12).

THE RIGHT TO NORMAL MARITAL LIFE

"Don't we have the right to take a believing wife along with us," Paul asked, "as do the other apostles and the Lord's brothers and Cephas?" (1 Corinthians 9:5). This raises the much-debated question: Had Paul been married?

This is probably a question that cannot be answered decisively. But there is presumptive evidence that he may have been married. He stated that when Stephen was condemned, he had cast his vote against him. This would imply that he had been a member of the Sanhedrin, a qualification for which was that one had to be a married man. If that was indeed the case, his wife may have predeceased him or left him when he embraced Christianity. But whether married or not, Paul asserted his right to a normal marital life, having his wife accompany him; but he added, "We did not use this right" (v. 12).

Many married people who are called to the ministry of the Word, either at home or overseas, voluntarily release their partners for longer or shorter periods, in the interests of the gospel. Others voluntarily renounce the right to romance and marriage so that they can give themselves with greater abandon to the ministry entrusted to them. Such costly sacrifices are not forgotten by the Lord, and they will have their own reward.

In the realm of romance Paul had his priorities right. To him the will of God and the winning of souls were of greater importance. His paramount concern he stated in a single statement: "to win as many as possible" (v. 19). All else must take second place. Romance in the will of God is wonderful but out of the will of God it is tragic. Experience proves that the crucial point of our surrender to Christ often lies just here.

When William Carey shared his missionary call and vision with his wife, she was totally unresponsive. He wept and pleaded with her in vain. At last he urged: "If I were called to government service in India, I would have to make arrangements for you and go. I am called by a higher One. I will make arrangements for you and go."

In the event, the captain of the ship refused to take him, and he had to wait for another ship. In the interval his wife changed her mind and decided to accompany him. Carey put God first in his marital relations, and God honored his faith and dedication.

Let it be said with all confidence that it is utterly safe to commit our plans for romance and marital life into the hands of the God who cares. For the single missionary this is often a recurring problem that needs sympathetic understanding. For a minority it will be God's will for them to remain single. Where that is the case only unhappiness will result from taking romance into one's own hands.

Here, as in all else, difficult though it may be, peace lies in the acceptance of the will of God. He never penalizes those who surrender their rights in this sphere.

THE RIGHT TO NORMAL REST AND RECREATION

"Is it only I and Barnabas who must work for a living?" (v. 6). The question here is the disciple's right to refrain from manual labor and, instead, be supported by the church as were the other apostles. Once again he renounced this right. "If others have this right of support from you, shouldn't we have it all the more?" he asked. Then he adds: *"But we did not use this right"* (v. 12; italics added).

There were cogent reasons for his refusing support from them. He did not want to be classed with the greedy priests who exploited their office to their own advantage. Then, too, he desired to maintain his own independence. He could exercise his apostolic authority more freely when financial considerations were not involved. Too often those who give the money want to call the tune. If he took no money, they could not dictate to him on matters of policy, and he would be freer to act in matters of discipline.

The principle involved here could be widened to include the right of the disciple to normal rest and recreation or the missionary to normal furlough. In Old Testament times God made provision for regular rest and recreation in the various festivals of the Lord. They were occasions for physical as well as spiritual renewal.

There is a place for recreation in the life of the disciple. A good test of the validity of our recreation would be this: Will it make me a better and healthier servant and a more effective winner of men?

Many Christian workers, including myself, have paid a heavy price for failing to allot adequate time for rest and recreation—as did the saintly young Scottish minister Robert Murray McCheyne. He lay on his death-bed when only twenty-nine, completely worn out by his unremitting labors. To the friend sitting at his bedside, McCheyne said, "The Lord gave me a horse to ride and a message to deliver. Alas, I have killed the horse and I cannot deliver the message!"

It must be acknowledged, however, that in the course of our Christian work, whether at home or overseas, occasions will arise when, in the interests of the gospel and the ungathered harvest, recreation or furlough will need to be forgone for a period. The disciple must hold himself in readiness to have his rights set aside where needs of fellow men are involved.

THE RIGHT TO APPROPRIATE REMUNERATION

"If we have sown spiritual seed among you, is it too much if we reap a material harvest from you? If others have this right of support from you, shouldn't we have it all the more? *But we did not use this right*" (vv. 11-12; italics added).

In support of his contention, the apostle cites the generally accepted principle that the farmer who produces the crop has the right to a share of it, as also the vintner his share of the wine. In other words, there is nothing wrong in being a paid preacher. Even the ox is not muzzled when he is engaged in threshing the grain. "In the same way, the Lord has commanded that those who preach the gospel should receive their living from the gospel" (v. 14).

Throughout his ministry Paul was meticulous in his financial dealings. He refused to allow monetary considerations to influence his decisions or actions. Money is an acid test of character. Our real riches are what go into our character, and these abide with us eternally. In his attitude toward money Paul was "clean"—something that cannot be said of all Christian workers. He had victory in the realm of finance, and he renounced his right to be supported by the church in order that he might win more souls to Christ (v. 12).

Whether we possess much money or little, it is our attitude toward it that is is revealing. There is no moral quality in riches or poverty per se, but our attitude toward it is a test of true spirituality. In a world in which material and financial values are paramount, it is not easy to escape their taint.

Discover a person's attitude toward money, and you will learn a great deal about his or her character. Not every Christian worker has mastered the problem of financial stewardship, and as a result many have lost spiritual effectiveness. Paul did not fall into that trap.

THE MOTIVATION

The voluntary renunciation of our rights in the four sensitive areas discussed above will require more than ordinary motivation and dedication. Some may find the price too steep and draw back. We should be grateful that Paul not only set the standard but shared the motivation that enabled him to make such costly renunciations with joy.

First, the positive factors: "That in preaching the gospel I may offer it free of charge, and so not make use of my rights in preaching it" (v. 18). "I have become all things to all men so that by all possible means I might save some" (v. 22). "I do all this for the sake of the gospel, that I may share in its blessings" (v. 23). "We do it to get a crown that will last forever" (v. 25).

He supports this positive motivation by strong, though negative, motives: "We did not use this right. On the contrary, we put up with anything rather than hinder the gospel of Christ" (v. 12). "I have not used any of these rights. . . . I would rather die than have anyone deprive me of this boast" (v. 15). "I beat my body and make it my slave so that . . . I myself will not be disqualified for the prize" (v. 27).

Taken together, these motives make a powerful appeal to the disciple who is zealous in the cause of Christ, prepared to pay the price of true discipleship, and has a passion for the spread of the gospel. In the history of Christian missions especially, we have not been without many whose renunciation of rights has paralleled that of Paul. Who will follow in their train?

15

THE DISCIPLE'S EXAMPLE

"Set an example for the believers in speech, in life, in love, in faith and in purity" (1 Timothy 4:12).

Paul was anxious that his protegé should develop into "a good minister of Jesus Christ." In his two letters to Timothy he aimed to brace and encourage him in view of his ministry in the important church at Ephesus, which was the most mature church to which Paul wrote. It had enjoyed a galaxy of talent in its ministry, including Paul himself. One can well imagine that the young man would have felt very keenly his comparative youth and inexperience and would have viewed his responsibility with trepidation. So the aged and experienced apostle gave him advice and encouragement that would, if followed, develop his leadership potential and further equip him for his strategic ministry. This advice is as relevant in the world today as it was then.

THE SEARCH FOR MODELS

"Exhibit in your own life a pattern of right conduct" (Titus 2:7).

In our times, when social structures are collapsing and home life deteriorating, there are a great number of confused young people who have no one to whom they can look as inspiring role models. They grow up with no father in the home, or no mother, and in a society that fosters sexual promiscuity, intemperance, and violence. As a consequence, they are unconsciously looking for models who will set an attractive example.

Recently I was startled while having a conversation with a friend.

"Do you remember when Hazel was in your office forty years ago?" she asked.

When I answered yes, my friend said, "Did you know that she was brought up in an orphanage? She did not know who her parents were, had never experienced love from anyone, and had never seen love between a husband and wife. So when she came to your office, she watched you and your wife closely to see if there really is such a thing as love."

Of course I knew her background, but never for a moment had I realized that all that time my wife and I had been under the microscope of a young woman desperately seeking a role model. I trembled to think what might have become of that young woman had we failed her.

How exhilarating it is to think that we can model the qualities of Christ to those who are searching for Him.

By an exemplary life-style, the disciple can make his or her Lord attractive to others. In his letter to Titus, Paul urged him to teach slaves to work to please their masters "so that in every way they will make the teaching about God our Savior attractive" (2:10). Obviously, our lives can make our teaching attractive to others. People should not only hear truth worth hearing but see lives worth emulating.

The word Paul uses in that verse is rendered *adorn* in the King James Version—"in every way adorn the doctrine." That word is used of arranging jewels in such a way as to show off their beauty to the best advantage. This is our privilege.

The private life of the disciple can neutralize the effectiveness of his or her public ministry. At a meeting I was addressing, a well-known archdeacon of a local church was present. At the close of the address he asked if he might speak.

"God has been speaking to me this evening," he said. "Most of you people know me, and I want to make a confession. When I am with you in public, I am always jovial and cheery and the life of the party, but at home I am a different person. I have been a street angel and a home devil. I have been bad-tempered and have given my wife and family a bad time. I have asked God to forgive me and to make me in private more like what I have tried to appear in public." His private life had been neutralizing his public ministry.

In his first letter to Timothy (especially in vv. 6-16 of chap. 4) Paul gave advice of timeless relevance to the younger man, and from it every disciple can profit today, whether in recognized ministry or in ordinary lay activity. "If you point these things out to the brothers, you will be a good minister of Christ Jesus," he wrote (v. 6). We will consider some of his injunctions:

TRAIN YOURSELF TO BE GODLY

We do not become more godly automatically. Becoming more godly rests in our own hands, and as Paul says, it involves training. As indicated before, the word *train* in the original text gives us our word *gymnasium,* and in this connection conveys the idea of "exercising the body or mind." J. B. Phillips renders verse 7: "Take time and trouble to keep yourself spiritually fit." The implication is that we are to be as eager to keep spiritually fit as the athlete is to win the Olympic gold.

Training involves regular strenuous effort, which will make demands on our time and activities. That is something we have to do. Above everything else, it will involve maintaining a consistent devotional life.

COMPENSATE FOR YOUR YOUTH

"Don't let anyone look down on you because you are young: see that they look up to you because you are an example to believers in your speech and behaviour, in your love and faith and sincerity [purity]" (v. 12, Phillips).

Paul was saying that Timothy need not feel his comparative youthfulness to be a handicap to his leadership. In any case, time would take care of that. Meanwhile, he could compensate for his youth by the quality of his life, by the model he provided for the church.

The apostle specified five areas in which Timothy should be watchful. These are areas in which younger people are sometimes deficient—speech, life-style, love, faithfulness, purity.

Although Timothy was not a mere youth, many of the elders in the Ephesian church would have been older than he. Yet he was not to allow them to push him aside as a stripling. He was there in response to a divine call. The tense of the verb gives the meaning: "Stop allowing anyone to push you round. . . . Give no one any ground by any fault of character, for despising your youth" (K. S. Wuest).

DEVOTE YOURSELF TO THE PUBLIC READING OF SCRIPTURE

"Devote yourself to the public reading of Scripture, to preaching and to teaching" (v. 13).

Timothy was to give attention to seeing that the three elements in the ministry of the Word were given due prominence. It is through the public reading of Scripture that the voice of God is heard. It is regrettable that that injunction is not more faithfully observed. In liturgical churches several readings from different portions of Scripture are read, but that is rare in many other churches.

The second element is preaching. Preaching is the exhortation that follows the reading of Scripture. To be profitable, truth must be acted on. It is spiritually harmful to repeatedly hear truth without responding to it. The exhortation will include advice, encouragement, and warning against error. In our day preaching has been somewhat downgraded in favor of dialogue, discussion, and counseling, but the injunction stands: "Preach the Word."

The third element is teaching—delivering a systematized body of teaching on the great central truths of the Christian faith. We are surrounded by a plethora of cults, and "correct theology is the best antidote to error."

Stop Neglecting Your Gift

"Do not neglect your gift, which was given you" (v. 14).

This gift of grace was the special inward endowment that the Holy Spirit had bestowed upon Timothy to fit and equip him for his ministry. We are not told what the gift was. The tense of the verb rendered *neglect* would give the meaning "stop neglecting," or "do not grow careless" about the gift. It would seem that the diffident Timothy needed prodding on this point.

It should be noted that the impartation of the "charisma," the spiritual gift, was not bestowed by means of prophecy but to the accompaniment of prophecy. The laying on of hands is always symbolic and not efficacious. The gift had been bestowed for the benefit of others; therefore, he was to keep on exercising it. By doing so he would demonstrate the progress he had made since he received it (v. 15).

BE ABSORBED IN THE TASK

"Be diligent in these matters; give yourself wholly to them" (v. 15).

He must throw himself into his ministry with abandon. A. T. Robertson says that "be diligent" here would be like our "up to the ears in work." No foot-dragging!

What end should Timothy have in view? "So that everyone may see your progress." His progress in holiness and likeness to Christ is to be so marked that it would be visible to everyone—to outsiders as well as to the church family. A convicting question to ask oneself is, Is my progress in the spiritual life so obvious that it is clearly visible to those with whom I live and work or to whom I minister? Or is my spiritual life static?

The disciple is exposed to two perils of which he should be aware. One is the danger of an unduly protracted spiritual infancy. Paul had in mind that possibility when writing to the richly gifted yet confused and spiritually immature church at Corinth: "I could not address you as spiritual but as worldly—*mere infants in Christ.* I gave you milk, not solid food, for you were not ready for it. Indeed you are still not ready" (1 Corinthians 3:1-2; italics added).

The second peril was spiritual senility. The writer of the letter to the Hebrew Christians was concerned that some of them had retrogressed into a spiritually senile state, so he gave this warning: "Though by this time *you ought to be teachers,* you need someone to teach you the elementary truths of God's word all over again. You need milk, not solid food! Anyone who lives on milk, *being still an infant,* is not acquainted with the teaching about righteousness. But *solid food is for the mature*" (Hebrews 5:12-14; italics added).

Timothy had to be on his guard against those perils and make steady and visible progress toward maturity (Hebrews 6:1).

DISPLAY CONSISTENT PROGRESS

"So that everyone may see your progress" (1 Timothy 4:15).

It is a salutary experience, as I know from personal experience, to take up this challenge and measure our degree of visible progress—or lack of it. One of the best measuring rods for this purpose is Paul's description of the fruit of the Spirit in Galatians 5:22-23. Let us embark on a voyage of discovery. Here is the standard: "The fruit of the Spirit is love, joy, peace, patience, kindness, goodness, faithfulness, gentleness and self-control."

Those delightful qualities, which flourished so luxuriantly in the life of our Lord, will provide us with a sure test of our spiritual caliber. Let us ask relevant questions such as: Am I a more loving person than I was three months ago? Has my progress in love been visible? Who has seen it?

It should be noted that the nine qualities are regarded as a unit, as, for example, a bunch of grapes. But love is the all-embracing quality. The succeeding eight are but different manifestations of love, which is the motivating principle of them all. Here is the checklist:

The first three qualities concern my private walk with God.

Love. There is no selfishness in love. The kind of love spoken of here is the unselfish side of life. It is more than mere human love. Rather it is the love of God poured into our hearts by the Holy Spirit (Romans 5:5). The Spirit produces both a sense of the divine love and the disposition to love God and others. It is an element that flowers even in the presence of the unlovely and hostile.

Can others discern progress in love in my life?

Joy. There is no depression in love, for joy is the natural outcome of love. Lovers are joyous people. *Joy* is more than vivacity and hilarity. It is the Christian equiva-

lent of the world's "happiness, having a good time." But
it transcends that by far, for it does not depend on *outside* happenings. Christian joy is independent of circumstances and can cohabit with sorrow. Paul said he was
"sorrowful, yet always rejoicing." A heart filled with the
love of God is filled with "joy in the Holy Spirit."

Do others see me as a joyous person?

Peace. There is no anxiety in love. Instead there is
an inner serenity and tranquillity—no borrowing of tomorrow's troubles today. Peace is love in repose. It is not
so much the absence of trouble as the presence of God.
Like joy, it is part of the Lord's legacy to His disciples. "I
have told you these things, so that in me you may have
peace" (John 16:33). When the Holy Spirit is *not* grieved,
the dove of peace is able to alight on the heart.

Am I making progress in the conquest of worry?

The next three qualities relate to my walk with my
fellow men.

Patience. There is no impatience or irritability in
love. Elsewhere Paul says "love suffers long." Patience is
one of the outstanding attributes of God, one of which we
have so often been the beneficiaries. It is not concerned
so much with what we do as with what we can refrain
from doing. "The strength of our love can be measured
by the length of our patience." This desirable quality enables us to bear with the foibles and failures, the irrita-
tions and idiosyncrasies of others even when we are
sorely tried.

Am I more patient than I was three months ago?

Kindness. There is no abrasiveness in love, for "love
is kind." It is a reflection of God's attitude toward us
(Ephesians 2:8). A kind person is sensitive to the feelings
of others and is always looking for the opportunity to
perform a kindly act, even for the unlovely and undeserving. Kindness mellows a word or action that might otherwise seem harsh or austere.

Am I developing a more kindly disposition?

Goodness. There is no depravity in love. Goodness tends to be a neglected waif in contemporary society. Goodness is not news. It is often snubbed and sneered at. If you want to insult a person, call him a goody-goody.

It is an arresting fact that when "God anointed Jesus of Nazareth with the Holy Spirit and power" (Acts 10:38), the outcome was said to be not ecstatic experience, spectacular miracles, or flamboyant sermons, but simply going about "doing good." Goodness is active benevolence.

Am I visibly a better man than I was?

The last three qualities have to do with my private walk with myself.

Faithfulness. There is no fickleness in love. This fruit is not so much "faith" in the sense of belief as "faithfulness" in the sense of dependability, reliability, trustworthiness—a quality that is highly esteemed. In a coming day the highest commendation of the exalted Lord will be, "Well done, good and *faithful* servant"—if we have indeed done well and been faithful in the discharge of our trust. Faithfulness has been described as the reliability that never gives up and never lets down.

Am I making strides in dependability?

Meekness. There is no retaliation in love. Meekness is not mere mildness of disposition. It is not a quality that is universally admired or desired, and yet the Master claimed, "I am meek and lowly in heart" (Matthew 11:29, KJV). Meekness is the antithesis of self-assertion. The meek person does not fight for his rights and prerogatives, unless a point of principle is involved or the interests of the kingdom are at stake. Jesus assured us that it is the meek, not the aggressive, who inherit the earth (Matthew 5:5).

Do I increasingly manifest a meek spirit?

Discipline. There is no laxness in love. Thayer-Grimm defines this quality as "a virtue which consists in mastery of the appetites and passions, especially the sensual ones." Paul employs the discipline exercised by competitors in the Olympic Games as an example of what the discipline of the disciple should be. Discipline is not the control of self by self! It is control by the Holy Spirit, who holds our appetites and passions in check as we yield ourselves to His control.

Do others see me as a graciously disciplined person?

Persevere in These Things

Perseverance. Paul's final exhortation was to perseverance: "Persevere in [these things]" (1 Timothy 4:16). That is, "Continue to focus your mind on holy living and unsleeping vigilance." If he perseveres in these things, the apostle says, he will "save both yourself and your hearers" (v. 16)—in the sense of helping them to be delivered from the "present evil age" (Galatians 1:4).

And what is the dynamic that will enable the disciple to continue making steady progress in the divine life? Paul gives us the cue when he attributes those qualities to the Holy Spirit. He produces the fruit in our lives as we live under the lordship of Christ. In 1 Corinthians 12:3 he says, "No one can say"—i.e., keep on saying—"'Jesus is Lord,' except by the Holy Spirit." If we are to make consistent progress in likeness to Christ, we need to be constantly filled with the Spirit, so that He can produce lovely fruit in our lives.

16

THE DISCIPLE'S LONELINESS

"You will leave me all alone. Yet I am not alone, for my Father is with me" (John 16:32).

Some degree of loneliness is natural and normal in the human situation. It is part of the human predicament. It invades the lives of great and small, and shows neither fear nor favor. The fact that one is a disciple of Christ does not put one beyond the reach of its tentacles, for it is endemic in the world.

Jesus, the Son of Man, experienced loneliness during His life on earth, and therefore there is no sin in being lonely. It can be classed as one of the sinless infirmities of human nature. So there is no need for the lonely disciple to add a burden of guilt to his pain. But loneliness can easily breed sin.

Loneliness has become one of the most pervasive problems of society, and its ravages have been exacerbated by the widespread breakdown of moral and social standards.

Loneliness is defined as "the state of having no companionship, being solitary, feeling forlorn." The very word is onomatopoetic, carrying with it the echo of its own desolation. It is no recent problem, for it had its beginning in the Garden of Eden. It is striking that God's first recorded utterance was to the effect that loneliness is not a good thing: "The Lord God said, 'It is not good for the man to be alone. I will make a helper suitable for him" (Genesis 2:18).

But later Adam experienced a different loneliness—the loneliness of sin. After he and Eve had fallen to the tempter's ploy, they were gripped by the icy hands of fear. Instead of enjoying uninhibited fellowship with God, they now knew the loneliness of alienation from Him, which is the most poignant of all forms of loneliness.

Loneliness comes in many guises. Sometimes it is like an inner vacuum, a sense of emptiness; or it is an acute sense of desolation; a deep craving for an ill-defined satisfaction. The loss of a close and precious relationship sparks one of its more distressing forms.

Contemporary social and environmental factors are one of the most fruitful causes. Chief among these is the loss of a life-partner, especially if there has been a long relationship. Moving from the family home that is too large after the children leave can be a traumatic experience. Removal from familiar scenes and friends leaves gaps and scars.

Almost everyone who is involved in a divorce or a separation—whether adults or children—has to tread the path of loneliness. It leaves an aching void.

Solitude Not Loneliness

It is wrong to equate loneliness with solitude. Solitude is something we choose, whereas loneliness comes unbidden and unwelcome. Solitude is physical, loneliness is psychological. Loneliness is negative and unproductive, but solitude can be constructive and fruitful.

It was when "Jacob was left alone" (solitude), awaiting in his tent with justified apprehension the approach of the brother he had defrauded, that he had his life-changing experience.

There are several levels on which loneliness attacks. The emotional level is perhaps the most distressing. The loss or absence of intimate relationships with other human beings creates a vacuum that is hard to fill. The only way it can be relieved is by establishing new in-depth relationships. To the person involved, that often seems to be impossible, but it is not. It will take a firm purpose, but it can be done.

On the social level, the victim may feel "left out" or "unwanted," with the consequence that he or she withdraws and loses touch with the community in which he lives. This is usually, though not always, a self-imposed isolation. That sense of social alienation or segregation is especially common among ethnic groups. Sad to say, it is not uncommon even in church groups, which should be leaders in manifesting the love of Christ and ministering to the lonely.

As has been already intimated, loneliness on the spiritual level is most desolating. It is isolation from God, who alone can fill and satisfy the human heart.

No Stage of Life Exempt

This malady of the soul is not confined to any one stage of life. In one of his plays, Shakespeare describes *The Seven Ages of Man*. With his pungent pen he delineates the characteristics of each stage of life with more or less accuracy. But one thing is certain, there is no age at which man is immune to the onset of loneliness.

Surprisingly, researchers have discovered that loneliness is much more prevalent in its acute form among adolescents and young people than among the old. Youth feels a desperate need to be accepted, especially by their peers, and they will do almost anything to win their approval. They feel "in between"—neither young nor old— and find it difficult to identify with either. That, in turn, causes them to resort to drugs, alcohol, or other hurtful habits.

Loneliness takes young people by surprise, but older people, although not welcoming it, are somewhat conditioned to the idea that it will come to them in some form sooner or later. They are therefore not so surprised when they have to face the reality.

However, older people do feel desperately lonely when friends and loved ones are called home one by one, or when children are far away and failing strength makes life a burden. They feel that they are no longer needed or perhaps no longer wanted.

One group that is expanding at a frightening rate is composed of solo parents and singles, who by choice live alone or have opted out of marriage. Our society is still couples-oriented, and people in that category often find themselves excluded from the social life of the community.

Single women who yearn for home and motherhood, but to whom the opportunity does not come, are in the same category. They tend to feel that they are regarded as second-class citizens. The Bible, however, lends no countenance to this idea. In writing of the single state in 1 Corinthians 7, Paul three times says concerning singleness, "It is good." His whole emphasis is that the single life-style is honorable and good; but not all singles share Paul's opinion. There is something to be said, however, for the view that with so many marriages ending in divorce and so many battered wives, "single bliss is better than marital misery." It should not be forgotten that a large part of the missionary enterprise is carried on by single women.

Divorce is essentially and inevitably a lonely experience for those who are involved. The pain is not over when the decree is signed; indeed, it has just begun. The world is full of lonely divorcees. One tragic side effect is that the children lose one parent—sometimes two. Inevitably that creates loneliness for the innocent.

The lot of the widow or widower is not enviable. Even when the marriage had not been ideal, there was at least some companionship, and the meal table was not silent. In the early days of bereavement, there is usually a great deal of support from friends and loved ones, but then life just goes on for them. Visits and invitations inevitably grow fewer. In many cases the widower is more poorly equipped to handle the changed situation than is the widow.

Bereavement is a desolating experience, and in the earlier stages one feels that the sun will never shine again. It should be accepted that it is not wrong or weak to grieve. Grief should be unashamedly expressed. Tears are therapeutic. Bereavement must be accepted as part of the human situation.

Although time does not remove the sense of loss, it does blunt the sharp edge of the sorrow. But immeasurably more potent than time is the comfort of God. "Praise be to . . . the God of all comfort, who comforts us in all our troubles, so that we can comfort those in any trouble with the comfort we ourselves have received from God" (2 Corinthians 1:3-4).

Some people hug their sorrow and, like the psalmist, refuse to be comforted, thus cheating themselves of the very thing they most need—the comfort of God. Jesus appropriated Isaiah 61:1 to Himself: "He has sent me to bind up the brokenhearted." Let Him do it!

REMEDIAL ACTION

Having reviewed many of the causes of loneliness, we now suggest ways in which its pangs can be assuaged.

It should be clearly stated at once that there is no simple and single panacea. Recovery from the condition will require wholehearted cooperation. There can, however, be an optimistic prognosis if the victim is prepared to take steps himself. Willingness to face reality and adjust to it is imperative.

There is hope of change only when the one who is lonely recognizes that he is responsible for change. One man's testimony was, "I realized that the only way to escape loneliness was through my own initiative." That was facing reality. There are certain things only God can do, and other things that only we can do. We are not robots. The attitude of mind and heart is vitally important.

Many proposed remedies are only palliatives, not cures—a travel holiday, another career, and so on. Such suggestions may well prove helpful, but they do not touch the real problem, for we take our lonely selves with us wherever we go. Frenzied activities will never fill the vacuum. To drop out of circulation will only compound the problem. Those alternatives are only Band-Aids on a broken leg. They may afford temporary distraction, but they do not effect a cure.

Most of us have at times found the medicine prescribed by the physician very unpleasant to take. But no mature adult would refuse to take the remedy simply because it was unpalatable. Some of the following suggestions may not seem palatable, but if the loneliness is sufficiently acute, the wise person will at least give some of them a trial.

1. Believe that the Lord is with you in your loneliness. Here are some relevant promises awaiting claim:

   > "My Presence will go with you, and I will give you rest" (Exodus 33:14).
   > "Do not fear, for I am with you" (Isaiah 41:10).
   > "They will call him Immanuel—which means, 'God with us'" (Matthew 1:23).
   > "God has said, 'Never will I leave you; never will I forsake you.' So we say with confidence, 'The Lord is my helper; I will not be afraid. What can man do to me?'" (Hebrews 13:5-6).

2. Since there is no sin in being lonely, don't add false guilt to your problem.

3. If outward circumstances cannot be changed, inward attitudes can and should be adjusted.
4. Don't constantly depreciate yourself. If God has accepted you, you must be valuable in His sight. Accept His valuation of you.
5. Clear the ground spiritually. If there is unconfessed sin, confess it honestly and fully, forsake it, and appropriate the forgiveness and cleansing promised (1 John 1:9). In that way you will get it out of your system. It will have the same effect on your spiritual life as draining a suppurating sore would have on the physical life.
6. Share your feelings, your struggles, and, yes, your failures, with your understanding Lord. "He knows how we are formed, he remembers that we are dust" (Psalm 103:14). Unburden yourself to your pastor or a trusted Christian friend and seek his counsel and prayers. A problem shared is often a problem halved.
7. Learn to live with some unsolved problems. Jesus told us to do this when He said, "You do not realize now what I am doing, but later you will understand" (John 13:7).
8. Abandon self-pity—"that dismal fungus." In many instances self-pity is the villain of the piece. To be sorry for oneself perpetually is a one-way ticket to loneliness. In one sense, self-pity is a denial of our personal responsibility to deal with the condition, and it frustrates the possibility of a cure.

   If we persist in focusing our thoughts on ourselves, that will only serve to fuel the fires of loneliness. If, instead, we turn our thoughts outward and begin caring for others, then our condition can be reversed, and we will be able to break out of the shell of our own desolation.

9. If circumstances cannot be changed, accept them rather than fighting against them; then adapt yourself to them and seek to adorn them.

ESTABLISHING NEW RELATIONSHIPS

Establishing new relationships is the real cure for loneliness, yet it is the hardest thing to do. But it must be done for the alternative is a continuation of the status quo. Here are some suggestions as to how new relationships can be formed.

1. Pray and look for opportunities to make friendly overtures to another Christian whom you think might become a friend.
2. In preparation for the approach, think of matters of mutual interest that could form topics of easy conversation.
3. Take the first step and make the approach. It will involve a definite act of the will.
4. Encourage the other person to talk about himself or herself. Show a genuine interest in the other person's concerns, and forget about yourself.
5. If you are shy and find it difficult to talk with others, think through opening and maintaining a conversation.
6. Remember that no single social contact will solve all your problems quickly. The fullest relief will be found in living fellowship with the living Christ.
7. Set your desires and ambitions on objectives outside yourself. Lose yourself in the interests of others.
8. Take the first step to break the pattern today. Don't wait for a more convenient time. It will never come.

In a meeting I conducted in Australia, a young man in obvious distress opened his heart to me. He had met with disappointments and had withdrawn into himself. He was desperately lonely.

I told him that he must take the first step and make the first approach if he wished for relief. I urged him to do it immediately. That evening he came with a beaming face.

"I've done it! I've approached my neighbor who has not been friendly, and he has promised to do Bible study with me." The Lord had answered his prayer.

17
THE DISCIPLE'S SECOND CHANCE

"The pot he was shaping from the clay was marred in his hands; so the potter formed it into another pot, shaping it as seemed best to him" (Jeremiah 18:4).

The patriot-prophet Jeremiah was heartbroken. Despite his tears and entreaties, his beloved nation had proven intransigent and was drifting further and further from God. His earnest endeavors to avert catastrophe had proved unavailing. He had exhausted all his own resources, and there seemed no alternative to deserved judgment.

It was just when he had reached this crisis that God gave Jeremiah a vision of hope. "Go down to the potter's house" the Lord said, "and there I will give you my message" (v. 2). Although Israel had persistently thwarted the divine purpose of blessing, if the nation would repent and once again yield to His touch, the heavenly Potter would make it into a new nation and give it another chance even at this late hour.

Although the vision was a contemporary message to Israel, the application is timeless. Just as the elements of the potter's art are essentially the same as in Jeremiah's day, so are God's methods and dealings with His children in every age. The context and trappings may differ, but the underlying principles are unchanging.

When Jeremiah went obediently to the potter's house, he saw the revolving wheel controlled by the potter's foot; a pile of clay inert and unable to improve its condition, of no intrinsic value; a pot of water for use in softening the clay and rendering it malleable; a scrap heap on which the potter cast the pots that had failed to realize his design; and, of course, he saw the skillful and experienced potter himself. "Then the word of the Lord came to me," Jeremiah wrote. "'O house of Israel, can I not do with you as this potter does?' declares the Lord. 'Like clay in the hand of the potter, so are you in my hand'" (vv. 5-6).

That assertion of the absolute, sovereign power of God sounds rather harsh and forbidding. His power is so final, and we are so powerless. But Isaiah the prophet softens the picture: "O Lord, you are our Father. We are the clay, you are the potter; we are all the work of your hand" (Isaiah 64:8).

True, God is sovereign in His power, but He also has a Father's heart. We can be absolutely certain that His sovereignty will never clash with His paternity. All His dealings with His frail and failing children are dictated by unchanging love.

As Jeremiah watched the potter at work, he saw:

THE VESSEL SHAPED

"I saw him working at the wheel" (v. 3).

The potter took a lump of plastic clay and threw it into the very center of the revolving wheel. Had he placed it a little to one side, the vessel would have emerged eccentric, lopsided. The spiritual lesson needs no emphasis.

Then, as his skillful fingers molded and caressed the clay, the pattern conceived in the potter's mind began to emerge. He shaped it first from without and then from within until the shapeless clay began to be a thing of beauty.

The potter was an experienced and skillful man. God is supremely skillful in the molding of human lives. He is no experimenter. He makes no mistakes. He never spoils His own work. The tragedy is that sometimes we arrogantly assume the role of the potter and try to shape our own lives, with disastrous results.

The wheel on which the vessel is molded represents the circumstances of daily life that shape our characters. How varied they are! Heredity, temperament, and environment are largely beyond our control, but they have strong, formative influence. God's providential dealings also play their part—adversity and prosperity, sorrow and joy, bereavement and sometimes tragedy, trials and temptations. All are factors that God uses to change us progressively into the likeness of Christ.

> He placed thee 'mid this dance
> Of plastic circumstance,
> Machinery just meant
> To give thy soul its bent,
> Try thee, and turn thee forth,
> Sufficiently impressed.
> (Robert Browning)

In the clay we can see our human nature. "You molded me like the clay," said Job (10:9). Clay is without value apart from the touch of the potter. Its paramount value lies in its capacity to receive and retain the pattern in the potter's mind. "It is the art that gives the value to the clay, not the material" (Dresser).

On one occasion I attended an art auction at Sothebys, the well-known art auctioneers in London. A small, and to me quite unattractive, piece of pottery was held up by the auctioneer, and to my amazement bidding began at £25,000! Then it rose to £50,000, £70,000, £75,000, and £78,000 when bidding ceased. The clay in the vessel would be worth a few pennies! The amazing value of the vessel to the purchaser had all been imparted by the touch of the potter.

A human life, like clay, has almost limitless potential when yielded to the heavenly Potter's touch. Why are some lives radiant and others drab? They are made from the same material. The difference is in the degree to which the Potter is allowed to work out the beautiful design in His mind.

There are endless varieties of clay, and each requires individual treatment, adapted to its texture and other distinctive qualities. So is it with the life of each disciple. Accordingly, God's dealings with each of us are unique and exclusive. There is no mass production in God's pottery!

THE VESSEL MARRED

"The pot he was shaping from the clay was marred in his hands" (v. 4).

As Jeremiah was admiring the emerging vessel, suddenly it collapsed into a shapeless lump of clay. All the potter's work had gone for nothing. The beautiful design of the potter was thwarted, and the prophet expected the potter to throw it on the scrap heap. We are not told the reason for the collapse, but it was doubtless due to some failure in the clay's response to the potter's touch.

Does this scene find correspondence in your life? The collapse was not due to any carelessness or lack of skill on the part of the potter. No artist spoils his own work. We set out on life with high hopes and ideals, but often we are worsted in the battle of life. The vessel is marred, but there is a bright ray of hope. The clay is still "in His hands." He has not thrown it on the scrap heap!

The heavenly Potter's design may be thwarted in a number of ways, the most common of which is the toleration of sin in the life. It may be open sin or sin cherished in the imagination. It may be sins of the spirit such as jealousy, pride, covetousness, or sins of speech. Those may seem more respectable than the grosser sins of the flesh, but they are no more acceptable to God. Sin of any kind will mar the vessel.

It may be resistance to the known will of God. The clay of our wills is too stiff to yield to the delicate touch of the Potter. A crucial battle often rages around one point of resistance—and that mars the vessel.

Or it might be some wrong or unhelpful relationship that is short-circuiting God's blessing.

These matters call for drastic action. They must be thoroughly thought through and ruthlessly dealt with if life is to get back on the right track.

THE VESSEL RESHAPED

"So the potter formed it into another pot, shaping it as seemed best to him" (v. 4).

Here is God's message of hope. Jeremiah's potter did not throw the misshapen vessel on the scrap heap, but of the very same clay, perhaps softened with some water, he made it into another pot. Such a pot may not have been quite as beautiful as that originally intended, but it is still "fit for the Master's use."

It was foretold of our Lord, "He will not falter or be discouraged till he establishes justice on earth" (Isaiah 42:4). Nor did He. The Scriptures are replete with illustrations of marred vessels whom He has remade.

Who but He would have chosen Jacob to head up the holy nation through which the Messiah would come? Jacob's very name meant "cheater, supplanter." Someone has said that he was so crooked he could hide behind a corkscrew. Before the determining crisis of his life, he had spent twenty years cheating and being cheated by his uncle, Laban. Then God maneuvered him into a corner from which there was no escape.

> So Jacob was left alone, and a man wrestled with him
> till daybreak. . . . His hip was wrenched as he wrestled
> with the man. Then the man said, "Let me go, for it is
> daybreak." But Jacob replied, "I will not let you go un-
> less you bless me." The man asked him, "What is your
> name?" "Jacob," he answered. Then the man said,
> "Your name will no longer be Jacob, but Israel, be-
> cause you have struggled with God and with men and
> have overcome." (Genesis 32:24-28)

Up until that time Jacob had resisted the Potter at
every turn and pursued his own devious way; but at last
he was defeated. He laid down the sword of his rebellion.
And God changed him from a cheat into a prince.

Simon Peter was not very promising material. After
many failures, he reached the nadir of his experience
when he denied his Lord with oaths and curses. When he
went out from the Lord's presence and wept bitterly, he
doubtless thought that was the end for him. It had been a
lovely dream while it lasted, but now he had "blown it."
He had better go back to fishing.

But the heavenly Potter was not discouraged. He did
not throw Peter on the scrap heap. In fifty days' time that
same Peter was preaching the flaming Pentecost sermon
that swept three thousand into the kingdom of God. Jesus did not even put him on a period of probation! "He
knew what was in man," and He saw the depth and reality of Peter's repentance. Not only did He reinstate him in
the apostolate, but Peter became its leader; he was entrusted with the keys that opened the kingdom of heaven
to both Jews and Gentiles.

John Mark was a promising young man who became
a dropout. When Barnabas and Saul set out on their first
missionary journey Mark accompanied them full of high
hopes and honored to travel with such men. But as opposition increased and the travel grew more arduous and
dangerous, his initial enthusiasm evaporated. He left
them and went back home (Acts 13:13)—a dropout.

When Barnabas suggested that they take him with them on their next tour, Paul would not hear of it. Mark had let them down once—no second chance. But Barnabas and the heavenly Potter did not drop him; they gave him another chance, and he made good. The dropout became the biographer of the Son of God! Marvelous grace of the undiscourageable Potter.

THE VESSEL PERFECTED

In His art, the Potter uses the fire as well as the wheel. Without the fire of the kiln, the vessel will not retain its shape. In the fire, moisture and unwanted elements are burned out. As the temperature rises, the clay becomes purer, and the beautiful colors of the potter's pattern are burned in.

What pattern does our Potter have in mind? It is no afterthought. Paul tells us what it is: "Those God foreknew, *he also predestined to be conformed to the likeness of his Son,* that he might be the firstborn among many brothers" (Romans 8:29; italics added).

Every touch of the Potter on our lives has that desirable end in view. The touches we sometimes fear are designed only to remove the ugly things from our lives and to replace them with the graces and virtues of our Lord.

> When through fiery trials thy pathway shall lie,
> My grace all sufficient shall be thy supply;
> The flame shall not hurt thee; I only design
> Thy dross to consume, and thy gold to refine.
> (Robert Keene)

The fire makes the pattern permanent. While walking through a friend's pottery, we came to the kilns where the vessels were to be fired. My friend made a remark that sparked a comforting thought. "We never put an article into the fire unshielded," he said. "We always encase it in a stronger, fire-resisting material. Otherwise the fierce heat would spoil the article." My thoughts went to Isaiah's prophecy in which the Lord said: "Fear not, for I have redeemed you; I have summoned you by name; you are mine. When you pass through the waters, *I will be with you. . . .* When you walk through the fire, you will not be burned; the flames will not set you ablaze" (Isaiah 43:1-2; italics added). We are never left to pass through the fires of testing alone —but do we always believe and lay hold of that fact?

The three young men, despite their affirmation of faith in God's ability to deliver them, were not spared from the flames of the furnace, but they were "encased" and shielded from their destructive power and in addition had the unspeakable privilege of personal fellowship with the Son of God. We do not always realize what design the Potter is working out in our lives.

King George VI of Britain was inspecting a famous pottery. When they came to a room where afternoon tea sets were being made, the escorting potter said, "Your Majesty, there is the tea set you ordered for the palace," and pointed to a black tea set.

On seeing it, the king protested: "But we didn't order a black tea set!"

"Oh no," rejoined the potter. "You ordered a gold tea set. Underneath that black substance there is gold. But if we put the gold into the fire unprotected, the set would be spoiled, so we paint it over with the black substance. When that is burned off, only the burnished gold is left."

When we are passing through the dark and testing experiences of life, we tend to see only the black. We forget that there is, underneath, the gold of purified character—more likeness to Christ.

After the series of devastating reverses and sufferings that overtook Job, he bore this testimony, to which numberless saints in subsequent years have subscribed:

"He knows the way that I take; when he has tested me, I will come forth as gold" (Job 23:10).

Judas persistently rebuffed the beneficent touch of the Potter on his life, with the result that there was no other place for him but on the scrap heap. Was it mere coincidence that the embezzler-suicide was buried in the potter's field that the priests had purchased with the thirty pieces of silver for which he betrayed Christ? His end is a solemn warning to any who, like him, are resisting the Potter's touch.

> Lie still, and let Him mould thee!
> O Lord, I would obey,
> Be Thou the skillful Potter
> And I the yielding clay.
> Mould me, O mould me to Thy will,
> While I am waiting, yielded and still.
>   (Author Unknown)

18
THE DISCIPLE'S RENEWED COMMISSION

"This is what the Lord Almighty says: 'If you will walk in my ways and keep my requirements, then you will govern my house and have charge of my courts, and I will give you a place among these standing here'" (Zechariah 3:7).

C. I. Scofield, editor of the annotated Bible that is associated with his name, used to tell of his resentment that every time he met with Dwight L. Moody, the noted American evangelist, he would pray that Scofield's commission might be renewed. He did not care for the implications of that prayer. But later he came to see that the clear-sighted Moody had discerned his Achilles' heel. Moody saw that with Scofield's intense preoccupation with the intellectual side of the Christian faith he was in danger of losing his zeal for God and love for his fellow men. Hence the evangelist's repeated petition for his friend.

Every disciple, especially those with a strongly intellectual bent, faces the same peril. We can learn valuable lessons in this connection from the manner in which the commission of Joshua, Israel's high priest, was renewed. Although the symbolic vision had primary application to the times in which Zechariah lived, it has a contemporary significance as well. Zechariah tells the story of the vision he saw:

> Now Joshua was dressed in filthy clothes as he stood before the angel. The angel said to those who were standing before him, "Take off his filthy clothes." Then he said to Joshua, "See, I have taken away your sin, and I will put rich garments on you." Then I said, "Put a clean turban on his head." So they put a clean turban on his head and clothed him, while the angel of the Lord stood by." (Zechariah 3:3-6)

The Disqualified High Priest

In vision, Zechariah was introduced to a scene in heaven. A trial was in process, with Joshua, the high priest and representative of his people, in the dock. Standing at his right hand was Satan, his adversary and accuser. To his dismay the prophet saw Joshua garbed in filthy clothes. According to the Mosaic law, that disqualified him from functioning as high priest.

The accusing counsel was not slow to make capital out of the situation and leveled his charges against Joshua. The accusations seemed only too well founded, for he offered no defense, and stood self-accused.

Suddenly, to Zechariah's relief and delight, the suspense was broken by the Judge's spontaneously intervening and rebuking and refuting the charges made by the accuser. Then "the Lord said to Satan, 'The Lord rebuke you, Satan! The Lord who has chosen Jerusalem, rebuke you! Is not this man a burning stick snatched from the fire?'" (v. 2). So Joshua's accuser was rebuked and silenced.

Next, as tangible evidence that the accused was acquitted, his filthy clothes were removed, and in their place he was arrayed in rich, festal clothing. His priestly commission was renewed, and once again he was qualified to minister before the Lord as His representative to the nation. Joshua—and in him the whole nation—was forgiven, cleansed, and restored to fellowship with God.

Because Christ has constituted us "a kingdom and priests to serve his God and Father" (Revelation 1:6), it is the privilege and function of every disciple to minister before God. In discharging that office, we may expect, like Joshua, to attract the hostile attentions of our adversary in his role as "accuser of our brethren" (Revelation 12:10, NASB). Joshua was doubtless one of the holiest men of his day, and yet when he found himself in the blazing light of God's holiness, he realized his utter unfitness to act as priest of the living God.

As representative of the nation, he was identified with them in their sin and guilt, and Satan had much with which he could righteously accuse them. Malachi the prophet records the condition into which the nation had fallen. So corrupt and avaricious had they become that instead of offering unblemished animals for sacrifice to God, they brought the maimed and diseased to the altar. Even Joshua's own sons had married foreign wives. Instead of rebuking and restraining them and lifting the nation to the divine standards, he had accepted and condoned their evil practices. Small wonder he had no answer to Satan's accusations.

THE ACCUSING COUNSEL

It is not without good reason that Satan is designated "the accuser of our brethren" (Revelation 12:10, NASB), for that is his favorite role. The noted infidel Ernest Renan termed Satan "the malevolent critic of creation." He is "the father of lies" (John 8:44), but he can speak the truth when it suits his plan. Whether false or true, he spews out his accusations against the believer, generating a sense of condemnation and effectively discouraging and unfitting him for service.

The devil delights to see a Christian "clothed in filthy garments" and, as he did with Joshua, he will do all in his power to prevent their removal. He knows that nothing can harm the cause of Christ more than a Christian who falls into sin. At the time of this writing, the whole evangelical cause around the world has been greatly harmed by the moral delinquency of some television evangelists, and Satan has gained a notable victory. But the final victory is not with him.

He is always on the alert to find something of which he can accuse us to God and discredit us before men. All too often we supply him with the ammunition. He is vastly experienced and knows how to exploit the weak spots in our characters, and he will stoop to any underhanded method to attain his end.

It is noteworthy that in Zechariah's vision the Judge did not deny the accusations brought by the accuser against Joshua and the nation, but He refused to entertain them. "The Lord rebuke you, Satan" was His rejoinder. "Is not this man a burning stick snatched from the fire?"

This latter is an interesting figure. Imagine an important document being inadvertently thrown into the fire. Just in time it is discovered and snatched out. The edges are charred, but the essential document is still intact. It is valuable though somewhat defaced. The fact that God troubled to snatch Joshua—and us—from the fire is our assurance that we are valuable in His sight and that He will perfect in us the work He has begun. "He who began a good work in you will carry it on to completion" (Philippians 1:6).

We should recognize that Satan has no right to level any charge against a believer. If you are troubled by his accusing voice, remember that the only One who has the right to prefer a charge against one of Christ's disciples is the One against whom he has sinned. That is implicit in the Lord's words to the penitent prostitute: "Neither do I condemn you. . . . Go now and leave your life of sin" (John 8:11).

Paul was reveling in a sense of complete spiritual absolution when he wrote the thrilling words: "Who will bring any charge against those whom God has chosen? It is God who justifies. Who is he that condemns? Christ Jesus, who died—more than that, who was raised to life —is at the right hand of God and is also interceding for us" (Romans 8:33-34).

When in a dream the accuser of the brethren confronted Martin Luther with a daunting list of his sins, he penitently owned them all as his. Then, turning to his accuser he said, "Yes, they are all mine, but write across them all 'The blood of Jesus, his Son, purifies us from all sin'" (1 John 1:7). That is the perfect and adequate answer to every accusation of Satan.

The Acquitting Judge

When God chose Israel as the nation and Jerusalem as the city through which He would bring blessing to the whole world, He foreknew their whole tragic rebellious future. Their actions and reactions did not take Him by surprise, any more than do ours. It was as though He said, "I chose Israel and Jerusalem knowing all they would be and do. I did not choose them because they were greater or better than other nations, but because I set my love upon them. No accusation you can bring against them will cause My purposes of grace to fail. Is not this a burning stick snatched from the fire?"

That is a message of encouragement for the disciple who has lost touch with God. Even with the memory of our most recent failure before us, it is still true that knowing all, God chose us before the foundation of the world (Ephesians 1:4). Although they have not surprised Him, our sins have deeply grieved our loving Father. But His foreknowledge did not quench His love. Because all the charges that could be brought against us were answered at the cross, He is able to rebuke and silence the accuser. True, we are just burning sticks snatched from the fire, but the Lord still has a purpose for our lives, as He had for Joshua's.

There is boundless comfort in the fact that although Joshua had a malicious and vindictive accuser, he also had an almighty Advocate. It is to our own loss that we so often listen to the voice of the accuser but do not hear the reassuring voice of our Advocate.

> I hear the Accuser roar
>   Of evils I have done.
> I know them all, and thousands more,
>   Jehovah findeth none.

THE RECOMMISSIONING LORD

There were four steps in Joshua's recommissioning and reinstatement.

He was cleansed. "Take off his filthy clothes" (Zechariah 3:4).

The words were addressed to the bystanders. Clothes, of course, stand for the character with which we are clothed. Filthy clothes signify impurity and sin in character. God will not rest, will not cease disturbing our lives until they are removed, and we should be glad that that is the case.

> Nothing unclean can enter in,
> When God in glory reigns,
> His eyes so pure cannot endure
> The sight of spots and stains.
>   (J. Nicholson)

It would not be sufficient for the old clothes to be covered with new, leaving the filthy ones beneath. Every sinful and disqualifying thing must be removed. Both Paul and Peter exhort us to "put off the old man"—the man of old—the nature we inherited from the first Adam. Doing that involves an act of the will, an act of decisive renunciation. We do not grow out of dirty clothes; we put them off. It is not necessarily a long, drawn-out process. It can be done suddenly and permanently. We can say, "I have done with that sinful habit, that doubtful thing, that unlawful association." When we take that attitude, we will find the Holy Spirit there to strengthen us to maintain that stand.

He was clothed. "Then he said to Joshua, 'See, I have taken away your sin, and I will put rich garments on you'" (v. 4).

Cleansing was the prelude to clothing. What balm those words must have brought to Joshua's troubled spirit, as every disqualification to further service for the Lord was removed.

The reference here is to the festal attire of the high priest. Removal of the filthy garments and cleansing from impurity were purely negative in significance. But God had something glorious with which to replace them—a wardrobe with rich attire suitable to fit and grace any figure and qualified to move in any company.

Augustine had lived his early years in sin and licentiousness, despite the prayers and tears of his godly mother, Monica, until one day he heard a voice say, "Take and read." He took up his Bible and read: "Let us behave decently . . . not in orgies and drunkenness, not in sexual immorality and debauchery, not in dissension and jealousy. Rather, *clothe yourselves with the Lord Jesus Christ,* and do not think about how to gratify the desires of the sinful nature" (Romans 13:13-14; italics added).

God spoke to him powerfully through those words. He said to himself, "I have spent all my time allowing the flesh to tyrannize over me, and now God has commanded me to put on the Lord Jesus Christ." By an act of his will he appropriated Christ as the complement of his every need, and from that very hour his life was completely transformed. The profligate became one of the greatest Christian leaders in antiquity.

God's wonderful wardrobe is at our disposal. It is for us, by a definite act of the will, to put off "the garments spotted by the flesh"—to renounce and have done with them. Christ waits to be appropriated to meet all our daily and hourly needs.

> Every need so fully met in Jesus,
> Not a longing that He will not fill,
> Not a burden but His love will lighten,
> Not a storm but His own peace will still.
> (J. Stuart Holden)

He was crowned. "Then I said, 'Put a clean turban on his head'" (Zechariah 3:5).

It would appear that up to this time Zechariah had been only an awestruck observer. But now, when he saw Joshua cleansed and clothed in rich garments, he interrupted excitedly and said, "Complete the restoration! Put a clean turban on his head!" He was referring to the turban of the high priest that bore the golden plate inscribed with the words "Holiness to the Lord." It was on this turban, too, that the fragrant anointing oil was poured. "So they put a clean turban on his head" (v. 5). The restoration was complete. His priestly authority could once again be exercised.

He was commissioned. "The angel of the Lord gave this charge to Joshua: 'This is what the Lord Almighty says: "If you will walk in my ways and keep my requirements, then you will govern my house and have charge of my courts, and I will give you a place among these standing here"'" (vv. 6-7).

The pardoning Lord had done His part magnanimously. It now remained only for Joshua to accept the charge, enjoy the privileges that were bestowed, and walk in His ways. In New Testament language, that would be the equivalent of "walking in the Spirit."

Joshua was not only recommissioned but was admitted to privileges he had never before enjoyed—the right of access to the immediate presence of God and admission into the very counsels of the Almighty.

19
THE DISCIPLE'S DYNAMIC

"I am going to send you what my Father has promised; but stay in the city until you have been clothed with power from on high" (Luke 24:49).

"You will receive power when the Holy Spirit comes on you; and you will be my witnesses" (Acts 1:8).

In these words, spoken before His ascension, Jesus urged His disciples not to embark on their public ministry until they were clothed—endued—with power from on high. He Himself had set the example. Despite His holy life, He did not embark on His public ministry until after "He saw the Spirit of God descending like a dove and lighting on him" (Matthew 3:16).

The disciples heeded His command, and on the day of Pentecost "all of them were filled with the Holy Spirit" (Acts 2:4). Until that time they had caused little stir, but before long they were being called "these men who have turned the world upside down." The dynamic power of the Holy Spirit transformed their ministry and made it mightily effective.

In these days when there is a good deal of confusion about the ministry and operations of the Holy Spirit, it is easy for zeal for opposing views to breed intolerance and to negate the spirit of love that Jesus said was the evidence of true discipleship. We should by all means speak

the truth as we see it, but it must be spoken in love
(Ephesians 4:15).

The Holy Spirit is not to be conceived in terms of an
emotional experience. He is not a mysterious, mystical
influence that pervades one's being; nor is He a power,
like electricity, which we can use for our purposes. He is
a divine Person, equal with the Father and the Son in
power and dignity; and He is equally to be loved, wor-
shiped, and obeyed.

There is a line of teaching that leaves the impression
that the Holy Spirit is a luxury for a spiritually elite group
of advanced Christians and that those who do not have
certain experiences are second-class citizens. But that is
a misconception. Indeed, Jesus taught exactly the opposite. Hear His words:

> Which of you fathers, if your son asks for a fish, will
> give him a snake instead? Or if he asks for an egg, will
> give him a scorpion? If you then, though you are evil,
> know how to give good gifts to your children, *how
> much more* will your Father in heaven give the Holy
> Spirit to those who ask him! (Luke 11:11-13; italics
> added)

In a parallel passage, Jesus adds, "Which of you, if
his son asks for bread, will give him a stone?" (Matthew
7:9).

Thus, in illustrating the nature and work of the Holy
Spirit, the Lord does not compare Him with the luxuries
of Eastern life but with the staple food in the everyday
Eastern home—bread, fish, eggs. Meat was too expensive for the average home and was regarded as a luxury.

So the point Jesus was making was that the Holy
Spirit is not to be regarded as a special luxury for the
spiritual elite, but like bread, fish, eggs, His ministry is
indispensable for normal Christian living.

The same truth emerges in Paul's conversation with
the Ephesian elders. He apparently detected a missing

note in their experience so he asked them, "'Did you receive the Holy Spirit when you believed?' They answered 'No, we have not even heard that there is a Holy Spirit'" (Acts 19:2).

After instructing them in areas where their knowledge was deficient, Paul laid his hands on them and "the Holy Spirit came on them" (v. 6). The Holy Spirit had already been given on the Day of Pentecost to the whole church, but the Ephesian elders had to believe that and appropriate the divine gift. That acknowledged lack accounted for their apparently anemic witness.

BE FILLED WITH THE SPIRIT

The command to be filled with the Spirit (Ephesians 5:18) is not directed to especially holy people, or to an advanced stage of the Christian life any more than bread, fish, and eggs are reserved for adults and kept from children. The Holy Spirit's gracious ministry is an indispensable and universal need at every stage of the disciple's life. Being filled with the Spirit is the indispensable minimum for a full Christian life. God does not hold His children to the bare essentials of life, but He opens to us an inexhaustible reservoir of blessing.

The tense of the verb in Ephesians 5:18 gives the sense "Let the Holy Spirit keep on filling you"—a continuing action, as foretold by the Lord: "'If anyone is thirsty, let him come to me and drink. Whoever believes in me, as the Scripture has said, streams of living water will flow from within him.' *By this he meant the Spirit,* whom those who believed in him were later to receive" (John 7:37-39; italics added).

What does it mean to be "filled" in this passage? We are not passive receptacles waiting for something to be poured into us. We are vibrant personalities, capable of being controlled and guided by the Holy Spirit—and that is what the word means. In Ephesians 5:18, "Do not get drunk on wine" is set in opposition to "be filled with the Spirit." In other words, "Don't be controlled by the spirit of wine, which produces disorder, but be controlled by the Holy Spirit"—bring your life under His control.

The same word, *filled*, is used elsewhere of being filled with sorrow or with fear—emotions that can powerfully control our actions and reactions. So when I am filled with the Spirit, my personality is voluntarily and cooperatively surrendered to His control.

It seems strange that although the twelve apostles had enjoyed three years of concentrated individual instruction under the peerless Teacher, their lives were characterized more by weakness and failure than by power and success. Pentecost changed all that; they were filled with the Spirit. After His Resurrection, Jesus assured them that that defect would be remedied.

THE PROMISE OF POWER

"You will receive power when the Holy Spirit comes on you; and you will be my witnesses in Jerusalem, and in all Judea and Samaria, and to the ends of the earth" (Acts 1:8; italics added).

A craving for power of various kinds seems to be innate in human nature. That craving is not necessarily wrong, but its motivation must be carefully monitored. Power is not always a blessing. Hitler had power, but because it was not matched by purity, and its motivation was terribly wrong, it plunged the whole world into chaos. The devil has power—"his power and craft are great" —but he uses it for destruction.

Two words are used for power: *exousia,* meaning "authority," and *dunamis,* meaning "ability, power, energy." It was *dunamis* that the Lord promised His disciples. He spoke of no mere intellectual or political or oratorical power, but power that comes directly from God through the Holy Spirit—power that revolutionizes life and energizes for effective spiritual service.

Note the change in the disciples after they were filled with the Spirit and received the promised power. It is recorded that earlier, in the hour of their Master's greatest need, "they all forsook him and fled." But now "they were full of power." "They preached the word with boldness."

In nature the laws of power are fixed, as for example in electricity. Obey the law, and it will serve you. Disobey it, and it will destroy you.

The Holy Spirit is the greatest of all powers, and He acts according to the laws governing His power. Obey those laws, and He serves you. Transgress them, and power is short-circuited. Peter underlined one of those laws when he wrote of "the Holy Spirit, whom God has given to those who obey him" (Acts 5:32).

Before Pentecost, the apostles' witness had made a minimal impact; but after that transforming experience, their words had singular power.

In his Pentecost sermon, Peter spoke with such power that "they were cut to the heart and cried, 'Brothers, what shall we do?'"

Words differ in their penetrating and convicting power. The words spoken by a man controlled by the Holy Spirit will produce conviction in his hearers, whereas the same words spoken by another not so endued will leave them unmoved. The difference is the presence or absence of "unction," the anointing of the Spirit.

In the experience of the disciples on and after the Day of Pentecost, we are given a prototype of the essentials of the filling of the Spirit. From that time on they had:

A new consciousness of Christ's abiding presence. In all their utterances and preaching, one gets the impression that Christ was just at their elbow. They were not reciting a piece, they were presenting a Person.

A new likeness to Christ's character. Through the now unhindered work of the Holy Spirit, they were being "transformed into his likeness" (2 Corinthians 3:18).

A new experience of Christ's power. When they conformed to the law of the power they craved but did not have, it was bestowed. Contrast "We could not cast the demon out" with "These men who have turned the world upside down have come here also."

One writer made the interesting observation that after the Pentecost effusion, the apostles did not rent the upper room for holiness meetings: instead they went out into the street and witnessed to Christ.

Just as there is diversity in spiritual gifts, so there is diversity in the manner in which the Spirit works in different lives at different times. In one person, the result is seen in a passion for souls; in another, an unusually voracious appetite for the Word of God; in another, a great social concern. But it is "one and the selfsame Spirit" who is at work in each.

Social Concern

There is a tendency to think of the ministry of the Spirit only in connection with spiritual activities. But a study of the book of Acts reveals that He was involved in the social and racial problems His disciples faced, as well as in their ecclesiastical and economic concerns.

Jesus required the anointing of the Spirit and power, not only for vocal ministry but also for going about doing good (Acts 10:38). The power of the Spirit is needed as much for service in home, business, and community as in pulpit and church. Many of the 120 at Pentecost are never heard of again. Doubtless many went back home to live normal, godly lives. God sees and promises to reward the unrecognized workers.

Stephen was one of the seven chosen by the apostles to oversee the distribution of relief to the poor Hellenistic widows in the Jerusalem church. The apostles recognized that that was a right and necessary service, and they delegated the responsibility to other capable men. That was not because they themselves were above such menial service but because they had a primary responsibility that they were not prepared to neglect—the ministry of the Word and prayer. Others could minister to the needy—God had given them that gift—but they had their apostolic responsibility, which no one else could discharge.

One of the qualifications for this social ministry was that the men chosen should be "known to be full of the Spirit and wisdom" (Acts 6:3). Stephen's faithful discharge of this hidden social ministry later opened the way for the powerful preaching ministry that culminated in his martyrdom. One of the important ministries of the Spirit is to equip the disciple for effective service in the Body of Christ.

There is one verse that holds great promise, but which, to me, appeared to be redundant. It is: "If you then, though you are evil, know how to give good gifts to your children, how much more will your Father in heaven give the Holy Spirit to those who ask him!" (Luke 11:13).

H. B. Swete points out that where *"the* Holy Spirit" occurs in the Greek, the reference is to the Holy Spirit as a *Person*. Where there is no definite article, just "Holy Spirit," the reference is to His operations and manifestations.

Thus in that verse Jesus was not encouraging them to ask for the Person of the Holy Spirit but for the operation of the Spirit they needed to effectively fulfill their ministry and do the will of God.

What a wonderful area of possibility this opens up to the disciple who is conscious of his own inadequacy.

Which operation of the Spirit do we need? Is it wisdom, power, love, purity, patience, discipline? *How much more* will your Father in heaven give that operation of the Spirit that is needed.

20

THE DISCIPLE'S HOPE

"The grace of God. . . . teaches us to say 'No' to ungodliness and worldly passions . . . while we wait for the blessed hope—the glorious appearing of our great God and Savior, Jesus Christ" (Titus 2:11-13).

Few intelligent disciples will challenge the contention that we are rapidly approaching the consummation of the age. Not the *end* of the age merely, for a campaign can come to an end with nothing achieved. *Consummation* means that the goal in view has been attained.

The New Testament constantly envisages the final triumph of Christ in time and within history. We are nowhere told to expect a cosmic Dunkirk, a rescue operation for a privileged generation. But we are encouraged to believe that there will be a complete world conquest for our glorious Lord and Savior.

The "blessed hope" of the disciple of Christ is not the rapture of the church, certain though that is, but "the glorious appearing of our great God and Savior, Jesus Christ." We humans are so self-centered that we tend to think of that glorious event in terms of what it will mean to us rather than what it will mean to Him. Even our hymns tend to be self-centered:

> O that will be, glory for me,
> Glory for me, glory for me.

185

The consummation of the age will be attained when Christ is crowned King of kings and Lord of lords and is acknowledged as such by the whole creation. It is toward this glorious event that the disciple's gaze should be directed.

SIGNS OF CHRIST'S RETURN

To a unique degree this generation has witnessed the universal and dramatic fulfillment of prophecy. Many of the signs Jesus said would herald His return have developed before our eyes.

There is *the evangelistic sign:* "This gospel of the kingdom will be preached in the whole world as a testimony to all nations, and then the end will come" (Matthew 24:14).

This prophecy has been fulfilled in our generation to a degree that has never before been the case. There is now no major nation in which there is no Christian witness. But as Christ has not yet returned, it is obvious that our task has not been fully completed.

There is the *religious sign:* "That day will not come until the rebellion occurs and the man of lawlessness is revealed" (2 Thessalonians 2:3).

Unfortunately, we can see this sign being fulfilled all around us. As Jesus foretold, the love of the many is growing cold (Matthew 24:12). But also in many parts of the world there is an unprecedented gathering of the harvest, so we do not need to be discouraged.

Political signs abound. Could prevailing world conditions have been more accurately and comprehensively described than in our Lord's words in Luke 21:25-26? "There will be signs. . . . On the earth, nations will be in anguish and perplexity. . . . Men will faint from terror, apprehensive of what is coming on the world."

There is *the Jewish sign:* "Jerusalem will be trampled on by the Gentiles until the times of the Gentiles are fulfilled" (Luke 21:24).

There are broad and general signs that Jesus gave to His disciples as precursors of His return. These and many other signs have been intensified and have come to fulfillment in our day. For the first time in 2,500 years, Jerusalem is not dominated by Gentiles.

Jesus reserved one of His sharpest satires for the Pharisees who demanded a sign from heaven to prove that He had divine approval:

> When evening comes, you say, "It will be fair weather, for the sky is red," and in the morning, "Today it will be stormy, for the sky is red and overcast." You know how to interpret the appearance of the sky, but you cannot interpret the signs of the times. (Matthew 16:2-3)

Whatever view we hold regarding the details surrounding the second coming of Christ, if we fail to discern in these broad signs an intimation of the imminence of His return, we should warrant a similar rebuke. History is moving rapidly—not to cataclysm merely, but to consummation.

CHRIST'S RETURN CONTINGENT

The fact that our Lord has not yet returned is a clear indication that the task committed to the church, to "make disciples of all nations," has yet to be completed. The uncertainty of the time of His return, rather than discouraging us, should spur us to more urgent endeavor. For His own wise purposes, God has chosen to make Himself dependent on the cooperation of His people.

Since, as we have seen, Jesus made His return contingent on our preaching the gospel as a testimony to all nations (Matthew 24:14), the responsibility of each and every disciple is clear. Peter spells it out for us:

> The day of the Lord will come like a thief. The heavens
> will disappear with a roar; the elements will be de-
> stroyed by fire. . . . Since everything will be destroyed
> in this way, what kind of people ought you to be? You
> ought to live holy and godly lives as you look forward to
> the day of God *and speed its coming.* (2 Peter 3:10-12;
> italics added)

The clause "speed its coming" is rendered "work to
hasten it on" in some translations. Any seeming delay in
Christ's return is not of His making. "The Lord is not
slow in keeping his promise," Peter assures us (2 Peter
3:9). The delay, therefore, must be due to the disobedience of the church, which has been slack in its response
to the Great Commission.

The above statement of Scripture could imply that
the date of Christ's return is not so inexorably fixed that
its timing could not be accelerated by the more rapid re-
ponse of the church to His command. If that is the case,
then the converse also is true—we can delay it by our
disobedience.

Scripture appears to teach that three things are involved in the timing of Christ's return:

The bride must be ready in some degree. "Let us rejoice and be glad and give him glory! For the wedding of
the Lamb has come, and *his bride has made herself
ready.* Fine linen, bright and clean was given her to wear.
(Fine linen stands for the righteous acts of the saints.)"
(Revelation 19:7-8; italics added).

It should be noted that this is something the bride
does in anticipation of the return of the Bridegroom. The
apostle John says the same thing in other words in his
first letter: "Everyone who has this hope in him purifies
himself, just as he is pure" (1 John 3:3).

Whatever else these verses may mean, a purging
and purifying of the church is in view. Who will deny that
the trauma and suffering of the last thirty years have not
resulted in the emergence of a purer and more mature

church in China? It is almost the antithesis of more afflu-
ent and indulgent churches in Western lands.

The bride must be complete before He comes. The
apostle John's description of the multitude assembled in
heaven is the picture of a group that is fully representative of humanity:

> After this I looked and there before me was a great
> multitude that no one could count, *from every nation,
> tribe, people and language,* standing before the throne
> and in front of the Lamb. They were wearing white
> robes and were holding palm branches in their hands.
> (Revelation 7:9; italics added)

Ever since the ascension of the Lord, the Holy Spirit
has been busily at work finding a bride for Christ, and He
has co-opted us for that privileged task. Not until the
bride is complete—that is to say, until the last person has
been won—will the Bridegroom come. The last stone has
yet to be laid in the building, the last soul has yet to be
won—and then He will come.

The church must have finished its task. This is more
nearly the case than ever before in history. It can now be
said for the first time that Christianity is known worldwide. But it is relevant here to ask the question: *Is the
task of worldwide evangelism possible to complete in
this generation,* thus to clear the way for Christ's return?
No previous generation has achieved it, so should ours be
the exception? I believe the answer is an unqualified yes.
On the first recorded occasion when Jesus made mention
of His church, He made a positive commitment: "On this
rock I will build my church, and the gates of Hades will
not overcome it" (Matthew 16:18).

God does not tantalize His children by requiring of
them something that is impossible to achieve. John Wesley said in this connection, "I do not ask if the task is
compassable—I ask only, Is it commanded?" Because Je-

sus commanded it, it is possible. Some generation, either now or in the future will launch the final assault on the strongholds of Satan and will achieve final victory. Why should it not be ours?

If we listen to the voice of history, the task of completing world evangelization (not world conversion) does not seem so impossible.

In 500 B.C. Mordecai the Jew succeeded in distributing the decree of King Ahasuerus, granting the Jews the right of self defense to all 127 provinces of the vast Persian Empire. It was a prodigious task. The royal secretaries

> wrote out all Mordecai's orders to the Jews and to the satraps, governors and nobles of the 127 provinces stretching from India to Cush. These orders were written in the script of each province and the language of each people and also to the Jews in their own script and language. (Esther 8:9)

But note the urgency with which the couriers executed the king's command. "The couriers, riding the royal horses, raced out, spurred on by the king's command" (8:14). When one compares this zeal and haste to obey the king with the lethargy shown by the church to obey the orders of the King of kings, it puts us to shame. They had none of our modern inventions—no cars or airplanes, no printing presses, no postal service, and yet they achieved this prodigious task in nine months! That helps to put the possibility of achieving our task in perspective.

When revival came to the little colony founded by Count Nikolaus Zinzendorf at Herrnhut, Germany, there were only three hundred members. And yet, when the count died, in a day when foreign missions were almost unheard of, the Moravian church had sent out 296 missionaries to all Europe, North and South America, Africa, Greenland, and the West Indies. In twenty years, they sent out more missionaries than the evangelical churches had sent out in two centuries up to that time. For one hundred years the Moravian church conducted an unbroken chain of prayer, day and night.

THE MODERN CHALLENGE

Why has God reserved most of the great inventions for this generation, if not to facilitate and accelerate the spread of the gospel? Think of the advantages we enjoy compared with all previous generations:

- We have almost total mobility. With the advent of the airplane, the world has become a global village.
- Radio, television, and other electronic media have brought the whole world within range of the gospel.
- Improved linguistic techniques have greatly reduced the drudgery of language study.
- Ill-health, which decimated the ranks of the early missionaries, is no longer as serious a menace.
- The church has abundant finance if members release it.
- There is an unparalleled reservoir of trained men and women.

Carl F. H. Henry, a well-informed Christian leader, maintains that seldom in history has the evangelical movement had such potential for world impact.

The task committed to us by our Lord is compassable. The motto that moved a previous generation of InterVarsity Christian Fellowship students to more urgent missionary endeavor—Evangelize to Bring Back the King —could well be revived.

Our generation will be without excuse if we fail our Lord. We must mobilize all our forces and resources and quicken the pace of missionary endeavor. The same Holy Spirit who empowered the early disciples to "turn the world upside down" is at work in the world today.

Ralph D. Winter, one of the best-informed missiologists of our day, is not pessimistic about the future of missions, although he is well aware of the adverse factors. He writes: "The world is about to see the most concentrated [missionary] effort in history. It will be the final assault by the most potent missionary force ever gathered. The modern-day battalions of William Careys will be made up mostly of young people."

Is the bride keeping the Bridegroom waiting because she is not making herself ready? Because she has not completed her assignment?

SCRIPTURE INDEX